ALPHABET STORIES

**Puppets and Picture Stories
That Teach Letter Recognition and Sounds**

by

Jill M. Coudron

Illustrated by

Jane McCreary

Published by Fearon Teacher Aids
an imprint of

 **McGraw-Hill
Children's Publishing**

Credits

Author: Jill M. Coudron
Editor: Bonnie Bernstein
Designer: Innographics
Illustrator: Jane McCreary
Design Manager: Susan True

McGraw-Hill
Children's Publishing

A Division of The McGraw·Hill Companies

Published by Fearon Teacher Aids
An imprint of McGraw-Hill Children's Publishing
Copyright © 1983 McGraw-Hill Children's Publishing

Send all inquiries to:
McGraw-Hill Children's Publishing
3195 Wilson Drive NW
Grand Rapids, Michigan 49544

Alphabet Stories
ISBN: 0-8224-0299-8

PREFACE

Alphabet Stories was written to be a companion book to *Alphabet Puppets* and *Alphabet Activities*. Together, the ideas and materials in these three books will enable you to teach letter recognition and sounds to your children through meaningful learning experiences in all curricular areas.

Alphabet Puppets introduces the idea of teaching the alphabet through puppets accompanied by stories, songs, cooking projects, and other varied learning activities. It provides patterns for making the puppets as well as ideas for incorporating the alphabet program into your classroom. It presents an effective method of teaching the alphabet that is stimulating for both the teacher and the child.

Alphabet Activities presents additional learning activities, which broaden the concepts introduced in *Alphabet Puppets*. It contains many new ideas for all curricular areas, simple cooking projects in which children are actively involved, and two reproducible activity pages for each letter. A wide range of activities is available to facilitate different teaching and learning styles. Incorporated, too, are ideas that enable teachers to work with children individually, in small groups, and as a class.

In *Alphabet Stories,* the puppets experience special adventures, which are pictorially portrayed. The letters and the sounds are carefully interwoven through the stories. Reproducible pages enable children to share the stories and puppet caricatures with their families, extending the learning beyond the classroom into the home.

CONTENTS

INTRODUCTION

Alphabet Stories is an enrichment and extension of my first book, *Alphabet Puppets*. The characters created in *Alphabet Puppets* now come to life through the magic of stories. Duplicatable pages enable each child to have his or her own puppet and its correlating picture story to use at home and at school for learning the letters of the alphabet and their sounds.

Each story contains many words and pictures beginning with a featured letter. The letter itself appears in the pictures in its capital and lower-case forms. Hearing and making the sound of the letter is an integral part of each story. For example, the children and teacher try to put out a fire by blowing the **f** sound during the tale of Friendly Frog.

How to Use *Alphabet Stories*

Duplicate one copy of the picture story on heavy paper to use in presenting to the children. Color the pictures attractively. Laminating the story cards or covering them with contact paper will enable them to withstand much more use.

After introducing the puppet at the beginning of the week, read or tell the story to the children, using the prepared story cards. As you finish presenting the cards, line them up for the children to see. Involve the children as much as possible in the telling of the story. Ask them to help you remember something that you have said already or tell you what they think might happen next. They should make the sound of the letter in isolation at its appointed times in each story. Encourage the children to add things to the story that begin with the featured letter and are appropriate in the context of the story. For example, in the story of Ditto Dog, the children can try to name more things Ditto digs up besides dishes, dimes, a doll, and dominos. Praise them for their efforts.

Make a special file box accessible to the children. As each puppet's story is introduced, place the stories in the box in folders labeled with their featured letter. The file box can be placed in a reading center to use for storytelling and sequencing. During their free time, children can take out these stories and go through them again and again. They can put them in order and

tell their favorites to you and to each other. Children can show the stories to parents and friends who come to visit the classroom.

As each week progresses, have the children cut out the puppets you have duplicated for them and attach them to a stick or straw. The puppets can be used for puppet shows, singing, and acting out stories; then the children can take them home to share with family and friends.

Ways to Use Duplicatable Story Pages

Duplicate the picture story for each child. Use one of the ideas listed below to work with the story. Vary your approach and methods of working with the stories to keep up the children's interest and enthusiasm. As you continue to work with the stories, you will discover the ways that are most successful with your group of children.

1. Cut out the eight story parts and compile them into a book. Construction-paper covers can be added and decorated. Show students how to staple their books or tie them with yarn or ribbon. Teach the children that books are bound on the left. Encourage them to "read" to each other and take home their books to share with parents.

2. Cut apart and glue or paste story parts in order on long strips of paper.

3. Glue or paste the story parts on a poster. When using this method, you can incorporate the teaching of left-to-right order in the placement of pictures in rows.

4. Make accordion-fold stories by folding long strips of paper accordion style and placing the pictures on them in order. These are especially fun for the children to use because they stand up.

5. Use the duplicated pages as they are. Have the children color the pictures or circle the items beginning with the featured letter.

Extended Learning Activities

1. Have the children find the letters hidden in the pictures of the stories. Have them find the things that begin with the letter. They can circle them, put an **X** on them, or color them a certain color. Try to use a color whose name begins with the featured letter.

2. Have the children act out the puppet story. Their involvement makes the stories more real to them.

3. Invite another class to your room. Have each child pair up with a visitor to tell him or her the puppet

story. Then ask each pair of children to draw a picture of their favorite part of the story together.

4. Hold an Open House for the parents and friends of the children. This can be an informal event in which each child acts as a spokesperson for what is happening in his or her learning environment.

5. Retell the alphabet story during the week. Children who missed the story the first day it was told will then have an opportunity to hear it. Let a child or a group of children help tell the story to the class.

6. Make a chart or list of all the words in the story that begin with the featured letter. Circle that letter in each word.

7. On a sheet of paper or in a little booklet, have each child draw pictures of the things in the story that began with the letter of the week. Help them label each picture and make a little ''picture dictionary'' for the featured letter.

I am Apple Auntie.

APPLE AUNTIE

1. Once there was a little boy named Andy. He loved adventures.

2. He liked sharing his adventures with his sister, Ann. One day Andy was looking all over for Ann. He found her in the kitchen making applesauce. She was wearing an apron with the letter **A** on it.

3. Ann and Andy decided to go for an adventure into the woods. Each of them brought along an ax to chop down things that might block their path.

4. As they walked along on their way to the woods, Ann and Andy practiced their adding. Suddenly they heard a strange sound: "A-ă-ă-ă-ă-ă-ă-ă-ă!" They looked around but could not see anything. They kept hearing it: "A-ă-ă-ă-ă-ă-ă-ă-ă!"   (*Have the children make the sound with you.*)   Finally, when they looked down, they saw what was making the sound.

5. Around their ankles were hundreds of ants! They seemed to be pointing with their antennae while making the sound "A-ă-ă-ă-ă-ă-ă-ă-ă!"

6. Ann and Andy followed the ants. Where could these active little ants be leading them?

7. At last, the ants stopped and pointed their antennae toward a cave shaped like the capital letter **A**. In the door of the cave stood the strangest woman Ann and Andy had ever seen. The woman said, "I am Apple Auntie. I live in this cave. I grow magic apples. Would you each like one?" Ann and Andy excitedly said they would love to try them.

8. When they bit into their apples, an amazing thing happened. The apples still appeared whole! Ann and Andy kept eating and eating, but the apples remained as though they had never taken a bite from them. How magical! Ann and Andy thanked Apple Auntie and the little ants for bringing them there, and ran home to share their apples and tell everyone about their greatest adventure.

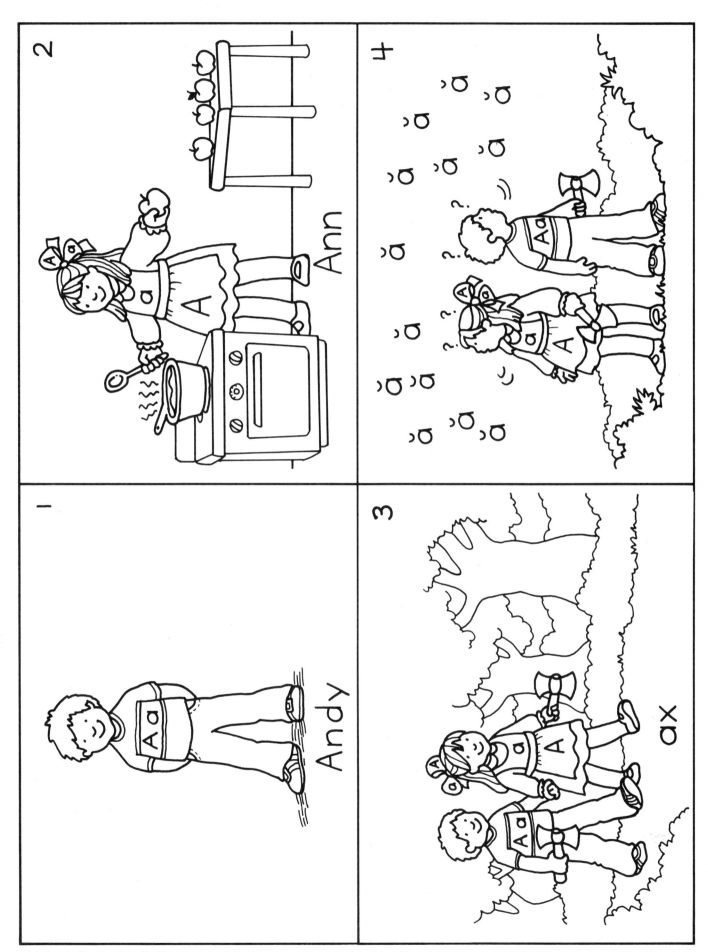

2

Ann

1

Andy

4

3

ax

I am B.B. Bunny.

B.B. BUNNY

1. Once there was a busy bunny named B.B. B.B. collected things beginning with the letter **B** in a big brown bag she carried on her back.

2. B.B. had balls, boxes, bicycles, bats, bottles, bananas, books, and baskets. She kept them in her big blue barn. B.B. didn't ask if she could take these things—she just took them.

3. B.B. became bored with collecting the same old things. One day she decided to start collecting things that were alive! First B.B. saw a beautiful butterfly. She called to the little butterfly, "Butterfly, Butterfly, I'm going to bounce you into my bag." The butterfly answered, "No, B.B. I WON'T be bounced into your bag!" But B.B. snatched the butterfly and bounced her into the bottom of the bag anyway. B.B. could hear the little voice calling, "B-B-But, B.B.!" *(Make the sound of **B** twice before "But.")*

4. Feeling braver, B.B. walked up to a bird. She said, "Bird, Bird, I'm going to bounce you into my bag." The bird replied, "No, B.B. I WON'T be bounced into your bag!" But before the bird could fly away, B.B. had bounced him into the bag with the butterfly. She could hear them calling, "B-B-But, B.B.!" *(Have the children name the animals in the bag and speak the dialogue with you.)*

5. As B.B. bounced along, she saw a bear on a box. She called to him, "Bear, Bear, I'm going to bounce you into my bag." The bear said, "No, B.B. I WON'T be bounced into your bag!" But before he could get off the box, B.B. bounced that bear into the bag with the bird and the butterfly. She could hear them calling, "B-B-But, B.B.!" as they bumped along inside the big brown bag on B.B.'s back.

6. B.B. began to get tired from dragging the bunch of animals in the bag. She came to a beach and decided to rest. As she sat there, she saw a big blue beach ball. It seemed to be alive as it bounced about. Every time it bounced on the beach, it made a tiny sound: "B-B-B-B-B-B." *(Have the children quietly make the sound of **B**.)* B.B. decided to take the ball. She bounced it into her bag and paid no attention to the bellowing of the animals: "B-B-But, B.B.!"

7. B O O M ! ! The beach ball burst! It burst with such a bang that the big brown bag burst, too! Bits were blasted everywhere on the beach. The butterfly, bird, and bear were blown safely into the water and they swam back to the beach.

8. B.B., however, had bumps and bruises on her bunny body. She was black and blue all over. B.B. said to herself, "That was bad! I'd better be a better bunny from now on." Because of this adventure, B.B. learned not to make others do what they did not want to do. Now everyone calls her "B.B.—the Best!"

2

bicycle

banana

basket

box

bottle

ball

bat

book

4

bird

1

B.B. Bunny

3

butterfly

6

B-B-B-B-B

beach   ball

8

bumps and bruises

5

bear

7

BOOM

I am Curly Caterpillar.

CURLY CATERPILLAR

1. Once upon a time there was a cute, cuddly caterpillar named Curly. Curly was covered with little **C** curls from her top to her bottom.

2. Curly lived in a colorful castle in Colorado. The castle was painted with all the colors of the rainbow. Cars came from all over to see the colorful castle that belonged to Curly Caterpillar.

3. There was one problem with the castle, however. It often was very cold inside. Curly was not comfortable being so cold and she would cry, "I am so c-c-c-cold!"

4. Curly would catch terrible colds. She cried and cried. She coughed and coughed. Her coughing sounded like this: "C-C-C-C-C-C!" (*Have the children make the hard* **C** *sound with you as they pretend to cough like Curly.*)

5. One day a caller came to the castle. It was Cousin Connie. She had come to keep Curly company. She knew how cold the castle was and had made some special surprises for Curly. Curly crawled over to Cousin Connie and cried, "Oh, Cousin, I have such a cough! C-C-C-C-C-C!" Cousin Connie cuddled Curly and told her she would do something about that right away.

6. Connie gave Curly the first package. Curly opened it and found a crocheted cape. It fit her perfectly and felt so warm!

7. Connie gave Curly the second package. In it Curly found a crocheted cap. Curly put it over the curls on her head. How cozy and comfortable the cap made her feel!

8. Curly thanked Cousin Connie for the crocheted cap and cape. She said that she would always wear them to keep from catching cold. Later, Cousin Connie and Curly Caterpillar curled up comfortably beside some candles and played cards together.

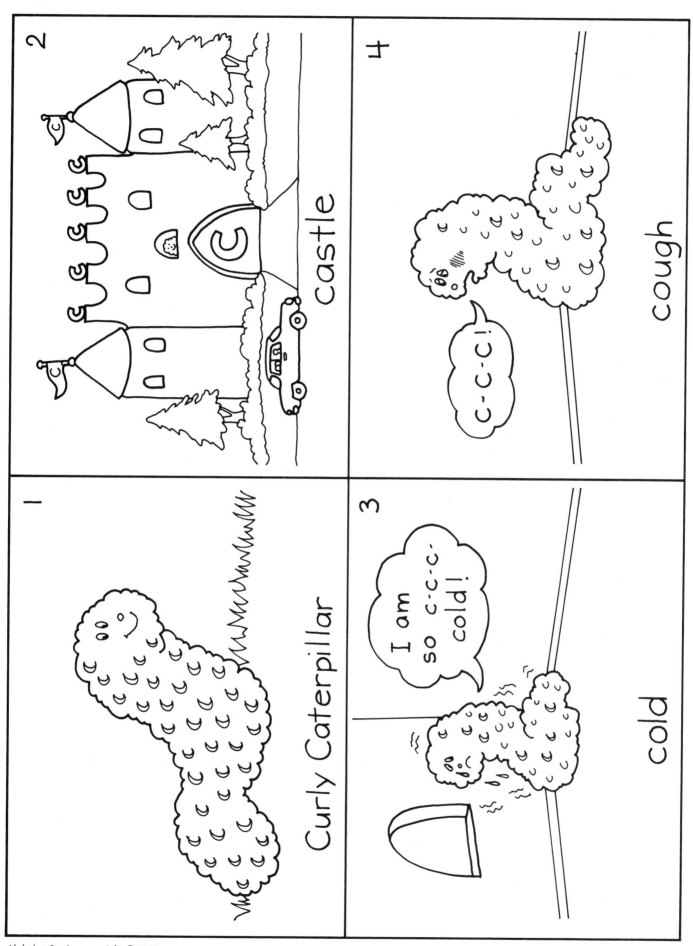

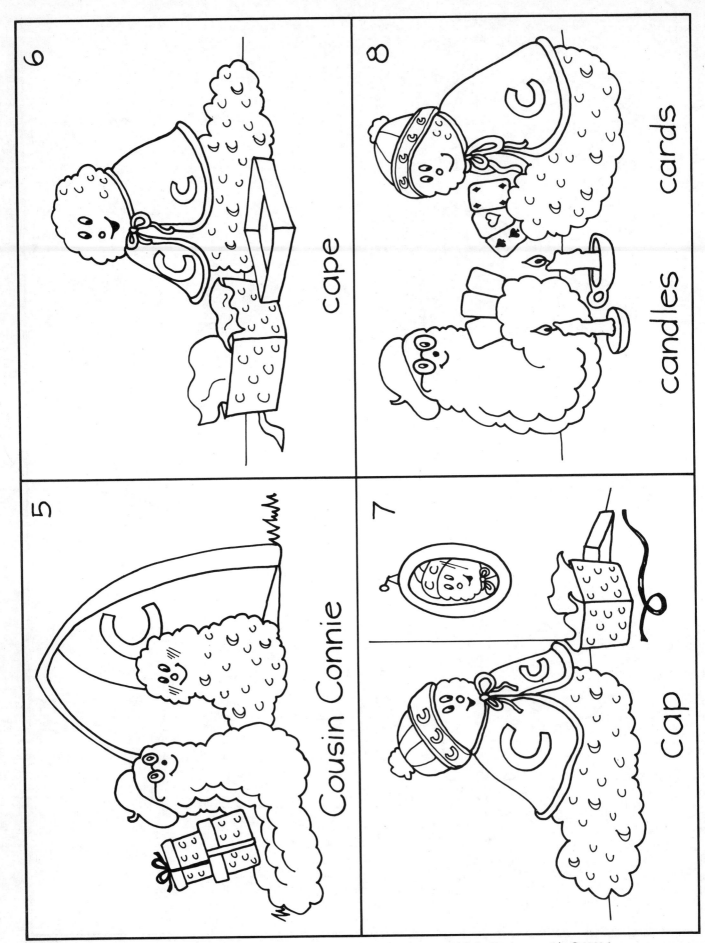

6

cape

5

Cousin Connie

8

cards

candles

7

cap

I am Ditto Dog.

DITTO DOG

1. Once there was a dog named Ditto, who was covered with dots. Since he loved to dig in the dirt, he would get very dusty and dirty.

2. Ditto lived in a doghouse near the driveway, with dandelions and daisies growing by his door.

3. Every day at dawn, Ditto began to dig. He could dig ditches deeper and faster than any other dog. One day while Ditto was digging, he discovered a set of dishes with **D** designs. He dragged them to his doghouse and decided to dig down some more.

4. Deeper in the dirt, Ditto discovered dozens and dozens of dimes. He was delighted! He dragged the dimes to his doghouse and set them next to the dishes.

5. Digging deeper down in the dirt, Ditto discovered a doll. Ditto dragged her to his doghouse and set her next to the. . . .   (*Have the children help here by naming the things Ditto has dug up already. Continue to do this as the story progresses.*)

6. Ditto dived back into the ditch. Digging once more, he discovered a set of dominos with dots. Ditto dragged them to his doghouse and set them next to the dishes, the dimes, and the doll.

7. Would Ditto dig deeper? Yes, he would. Ditto dropped into the ditch and dug and dug and dug. It was growing dark inside the ditch, since Ditto had dug down SO far. Ditto heard a faint noise: "D-D-D-D-D."
    (*Have the children make the sound of **D** with you.*)   He kept digging toward the sound "D-D-D-D-D." Louder and louder it became—"D! D! D! D! D!"—until Ditto found, of all things, a dinosaur!

8. Ditto and the dinosaur became good friends. They played with the dishes, doll, and dominos. They spent the dimes on dinners, desserts, and dances. They enjoyed dancing as they hummed like this: "D-D-D-D-D."

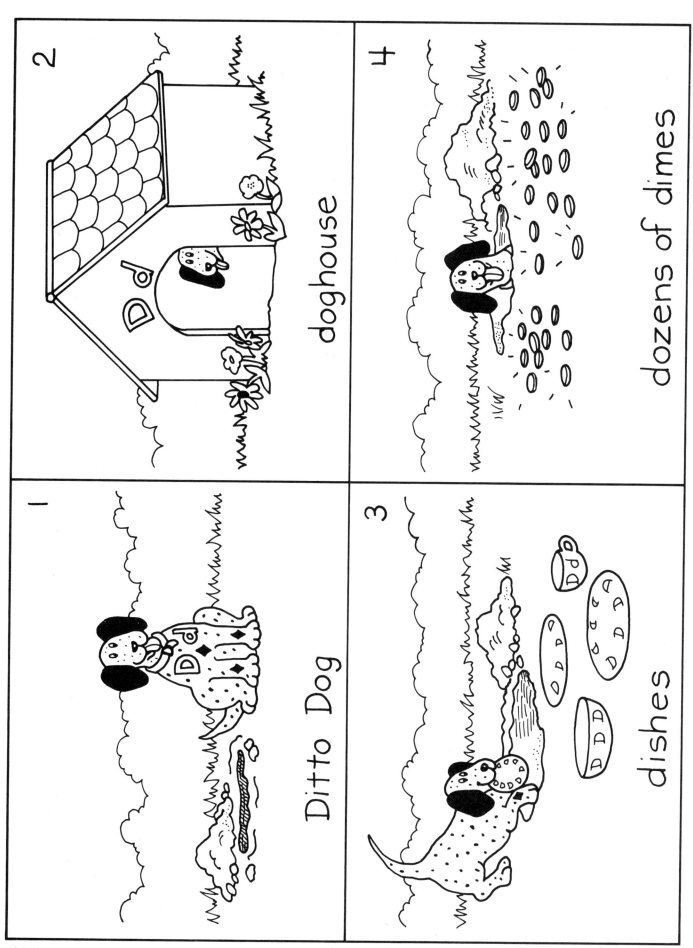

2

doghouse

1

Ditto Dog

4

dozens of dimes

3

dishes

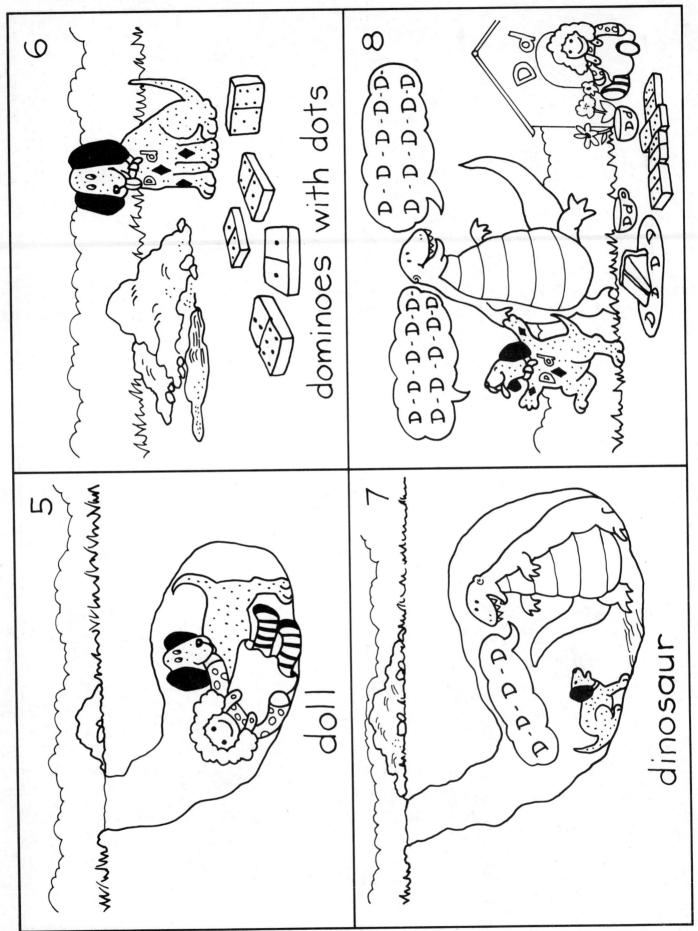

6

dominoes with dots

5

doll

8

7

dinosaur

18

I am Enor Elephant.

ENOR ELEPHANT

1. Once upon a time there was an elephant named Enor. Because he had ENORMOUS eyes, he could see extremely well. Because he had ENORMOUS ears, he could hear extremely well. And because he did exercises, he had an ENORMOUS amount of energy.

2. Enor was the captain of the Elephants-Eleven Emergency Team. They were a group of elephants that were experts in emergencies. To show everyone they were part of the team, they always wore this emblem: E-11-e.

3. Enor had taught all the people and animals around to make a certain sound when they were in trouble and needed help. When his enormous ears would hear that sound, his enormous eyes would help find whoever was in trouble. The sound was this: "E-ĕ-ĕ-ĕ-ĕ-ĕ-ĕ-ĕ-ĕ-ĕ-ĕ." (*Say the sound of short* **e** *four times, then say the name of letter* **E** *four times, and then repeat the short* **e** *sound four times.*)

4. When Enor heard the sound, he would echo it. The other elephants from the emergency team would hurry to help. They would follow the sound "E-ĕ-ĕ-ĕ-ĕ-ĕ-ĕ-ĕ-ĕ-ĕ-ĕ." (*Have the children make the sound with you throughout the story.*)

5. Upon entering a forest early one day, the Elephants-Eleven helped a family of elks that had been trapped by an explosion. The team had heard the elks calling: "E-ĕ-ĕ-ĕ-ĕ-ĕ-ĕ-ĕ-ĕ-ĕ-ĕ." The elephants helped them escape.

6. Another time they had heard a tiny call for help: "E-ĕ-ĕ-ĕ-ĕ-ĕ-ĕ-ĕ-ĕ-ĕ-ĕ." It was an elf trapped in an elevator. They got her out, too.

7. Once they heard the call from exhausted Eskimos who had been experimenting with an engine. The elephants got the engine running so the Eskimos could go home.

8. The Elephants-Eleven, with Enor as their leader, helped many people and animals in emergencies. Be sure to remember their echo code if YOU ever have an emergency: "E-ĕ-ĕ-ĕ-ĕ-ĕ-ĕ-ĕ-ĕ-ĕ-ĕ."

2

E-ll-e

Elephants-Eleven

4

E e

1

E e

Enor Elephant

3

E e

echo

6

elf in an elevator

5

elks

8

emergency

7

Eskimos with an engine

I am Friendly Frog.

FRIENDLY FROG

1. Once in a faraway field there lived a fine fat frog named Friendly. He liked to be funny and do flip-flops. Can you do a flip-flop? It's fun!

2. Friendly had a friend named Fancy Fish. They were always together finding fun things to do. They both had freckles.

3. Friendly liked to take Fancy on walks in the forest. Ttey had found fantastic things in the forest. Their favorites were flowers, fossils, and feathers.

4. One day while they were wandering far into the forest, they saw flames from a forest fire! They knew this was a frightful, dangerous thing. They ran to fight the fire.

5. As they got closer to the fire, they heard voices calling out, "Fire! fire! Find us, please!" They knew they had to find whoever was there.

6. Finally they found who the voices belonged to: a family of five foxes that was trapped by the fire. The foxes continued to call out, "Fire! Fire! Find us, please!" Friendly called back to them, "Don't be frightened. I'll save you fine foxes!"

7. Friendly blew on the fire in a special way as hard as he could. Fancy helped her friend: "F-F-F-F-F-F-F-F-F-F-F-F-F-F-F-F-F-F-F-F-F!" (*Have the children make a continuous sound of* **F** *with you to "help blow out" the fire.*)   Finally, Friendly and Fancy had blown out all the flames. The five foxes were saved!

8. Friendly and Fancy led the tired, frightened foxes back to Friendly's farm. They fixed fantastic flapjacks for the foxes. Each fox ate four flapjacks. They ate them fast, fast, fast! Fancy, Friendly, and the five foxes became fine friends. They often were seen frolicking in the forest. Friendly taught everyone how to do flip-flops. What fun!

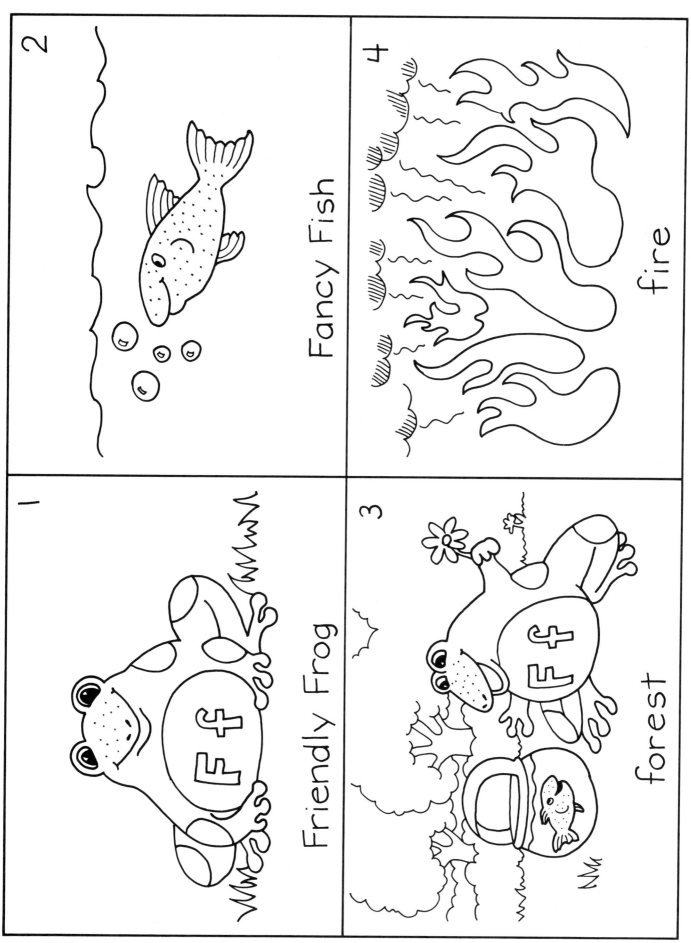

2

Fancy Fish

4

fire

1

Friendly Frog

3

forest

6

five foxes

8

Friendly's farm
Ff

flapjacks

5

Fire! Fire!
Find us, please!

7

F-F-F-F-
F-F-F-F-
F-F-F-F-
F-F-F-F-
F-F-F-F-
F-F-F-F-

26 *Alphabet Stories* copyright © 1983

I am Goofy Ghost.

GOOFY GHOST

1. This is the story of Goofy Ghost. Goofy is a green ghost with glasses. He lives in a green garbage can painted with gold **G**s. He is a great ghost because he glides in and out of the garbage can so easily.

2. Goofy loves to play the guitar. He plays it in the garbage can sometimes, but he also likes to play at the grocery store. He makes a gurgling sound when he sings, like this: "G-G-G-G-G-G-G." (*Have the children make the hard **G** sound here and throughout the story.*)

3. Goofy, being a ghost, likes to scare people. But he has his own special way to do this. Most ghosts say, "BOO!" But not Goofy. He says very loudly, "G-G-G-GOO!"

4. Goofy is forever gliding off somewhere to scare someone. You never know where he will turn up. He likes going to the gas station to let out a scary "G-G-G-GOO!" When people figure out who he is, they say, "Good grief, Goofy!"

5. Sometimes Goofy goes to the golf course to scare the golfers with a loud "G-G-G-GOO!" The golfers cry out, "Good grief, Goofy!"

6. Sometimes Goofy goes to people's garages to scare them when they come home in their cars. He glides right under the door, and when they come home, he is all ready with his "G-G-G-GOO!" They jump in fright and say, "Good grief, Goofy!"

7. Goofy likes to do the ghost gallop around people's gardens. He goes behind bushes and flowers and is all ready to surprise someone with his "G-G-G-GOO!"

8. After doing a good job being a ghost, Goofy gaily goes back to his green garbage can, feeling great. Good night, Goofy!

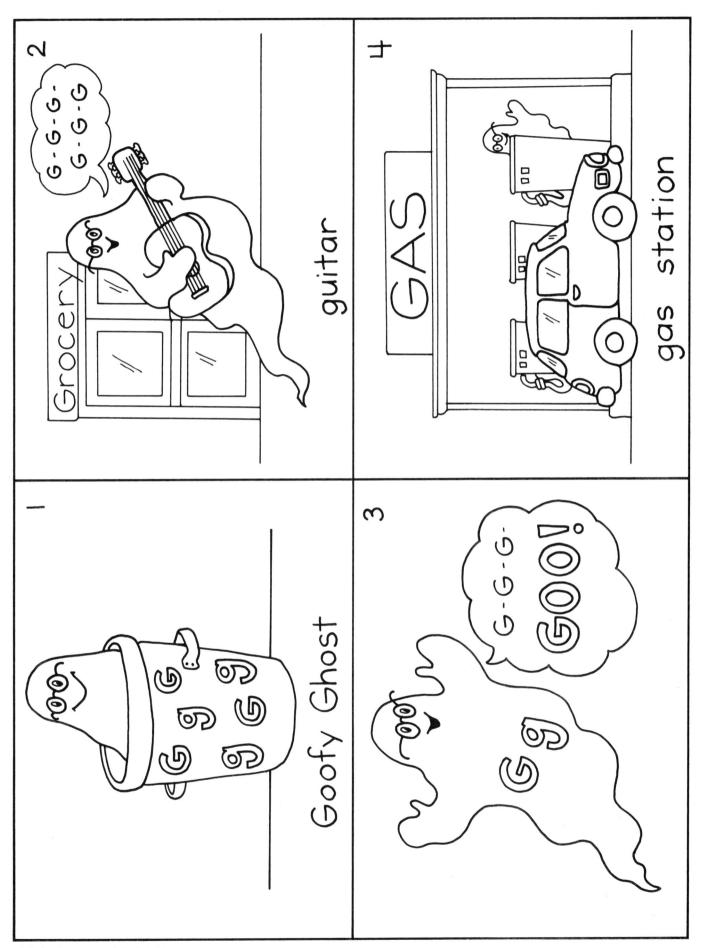

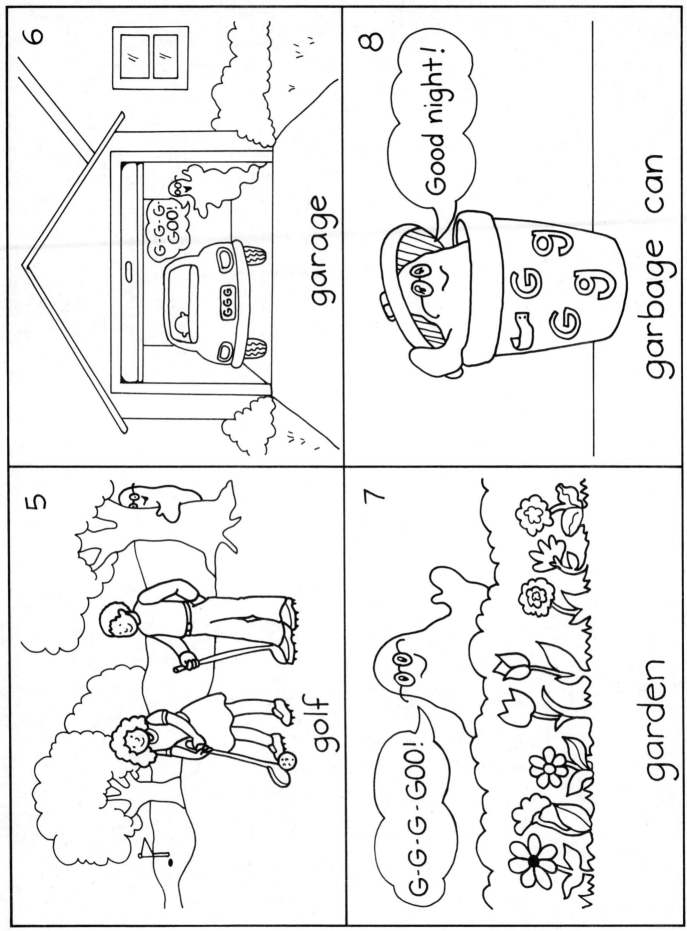

I am Happy Hippo.

HAPPY HIPPO

1. Once upon a time there was a hippo named Happy. Happy was a heavy hippo with two horns, lots of hair, a hook holding a hanky, and a kind heart.

2. Happy lived with a herd of hippos in a hippo house shaped like the letter **H**. Because the hippos were so heavy, each had his or her own heap of hay. When all the hippos were asleep on their heaps of hay, they made this sound: "H-H-H-H-H." Can you make that hippo sound?   (*Repeat the sound of the letter* **H**.)

3. Happy had a hobby of collecting all kinds of hats. He had hundreds and hundreds of hats hanging around his area of the hippo house.

4. One day Happy met a new friend, Hannah Hippo. She lived in another hippo house. Hannah invited Happy to come to her house for a special treat to celebrate Hippopotamus Holiday. The treat was hamburgers!

5. Happy was very excited. As he began to get ready, he laughed, "Ho, ho, ho!" He had to find just the right hat, however. Which one would it be? He began to take all the hats off their hooks to try them on. No, this hat was too HARD. This one was too HOT.

6. The next hat was just too HUGE. This one was too HIGH.

7. The HAMMER hat was just not right for hamburgers. And this hat was just too HEAVY! "Help!" said Happy. "I'm hungry! I have to hurry!" Hannah's hamburgers were almost ready.

8. Finally Happy picked up his "happy hat." It fit him perfectly and looked just right. Happy said, "I sure hope that Hannah will like my happy hat!" She did, and together they had heavenly hamburgers and a happy holiday.

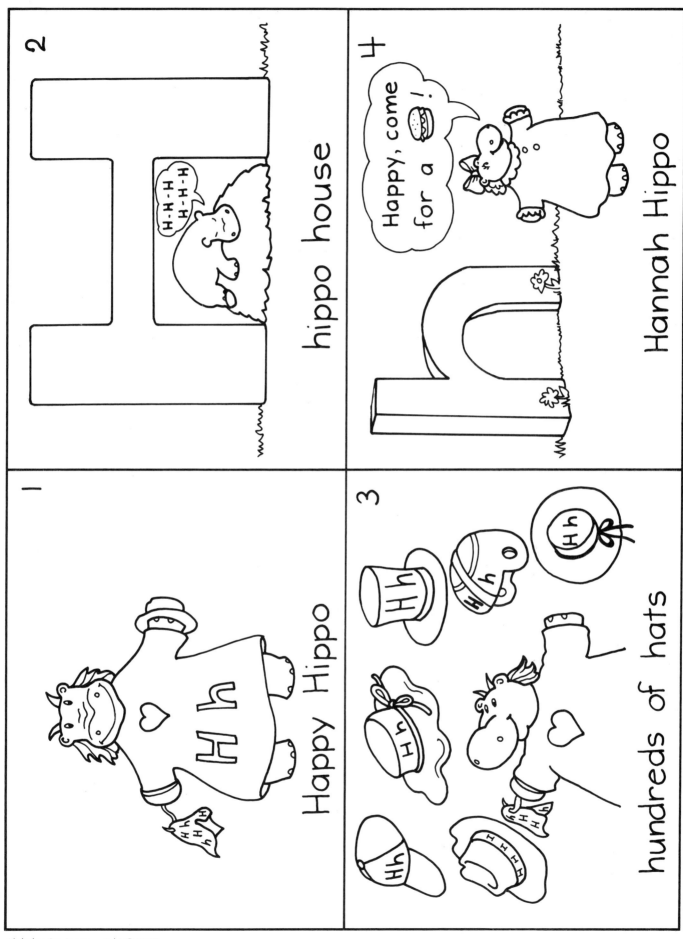

2

hippo house

4

Happy, come for a ___!

Hannah Hippo

1

Happy Hippo

3

hundreds of hats

33

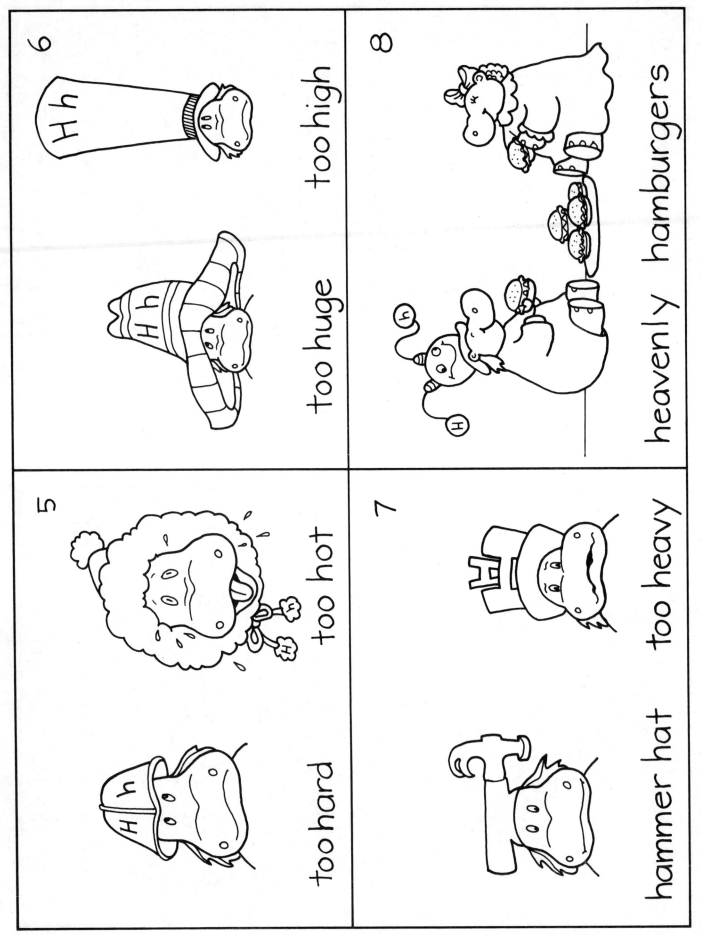

6

too high

too huge

8

heavenly hamburgers

5

too hot

too hard

7

too heavy

hammer hat

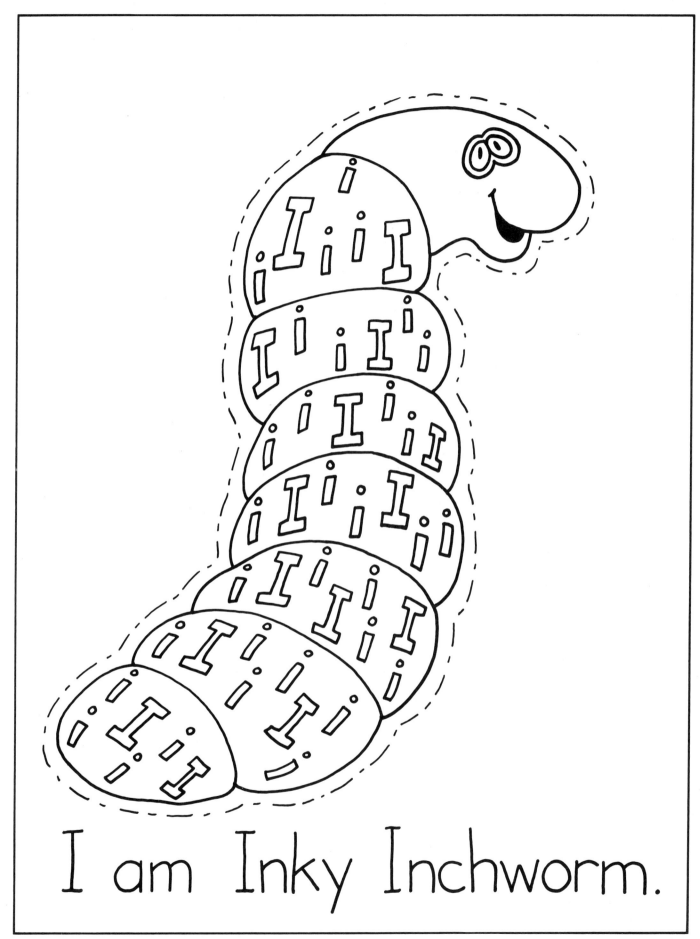

I am Inky Inchworm.

INKY INCHWORM

1. Once upon a time there was an inchworm named Inky. There were many things in Inky's life that made life impossible for him. This is the story of Inky's troubles.

2. Inky lived in an inn, which is like a hotel. Anyone would think an inn was a nice place to live, but it was not nice for Inky.

3. The inn was full of other insects. When Inky became upset with their creeping and crawling around, he would shake his hands and say, "Icky, icky, icky!"   (*Have the children make this motion and say these words with you throughout the story.*)

4. Also staying at the inn were infants, who cried and fussed all the time. When Inky became upset with their noise, he would call out, "Icky, icky, icky!"

5. As if the insects and infants were not enough for poor Inky, there was a band that played instruments at the inn. My, the noise they made was intolerable! When the instruments disturbed his days and nights, Inky would cry out, "Icky, icky, icky!"

6. One afternoon while Inky was imagining what life would be like without insects, infants, and instruments, an important Eskimo named Ivan walked over to him and asked, "What's the matter, little inchworm? You look so sad." Inky told Ivan how the insects, infants, and instruments were making his life so imposible. Ivan and Inky said, "Icky, icky, icky!" Then Ivan told Inky about an interesting idea he had.

7. Inky and Ivan went outdoors and began to collect blocks of ice. Together they built a special place called an igloo. It made a lovely home for Inky. It was peaceful and quiet, and there were no insects, infants, or instruments to disturb him.

8. Inky thanked Ivan for helping him by inviting him into the igloo for ice cream. Inky lived happily ever after in his igloo.

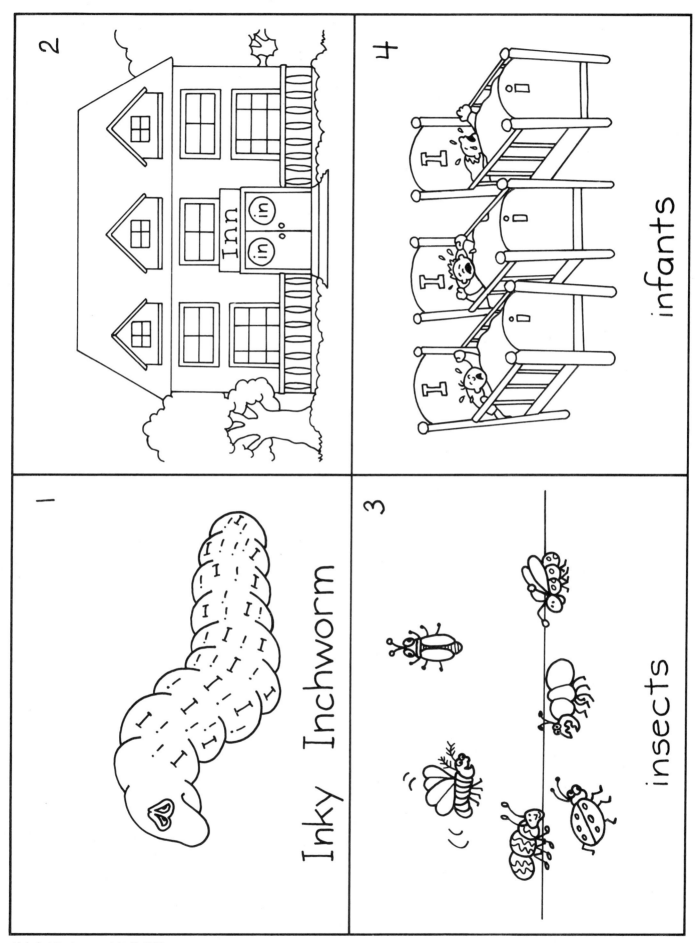

2

1

Inky Inchworm

4

infants

3

insects

37

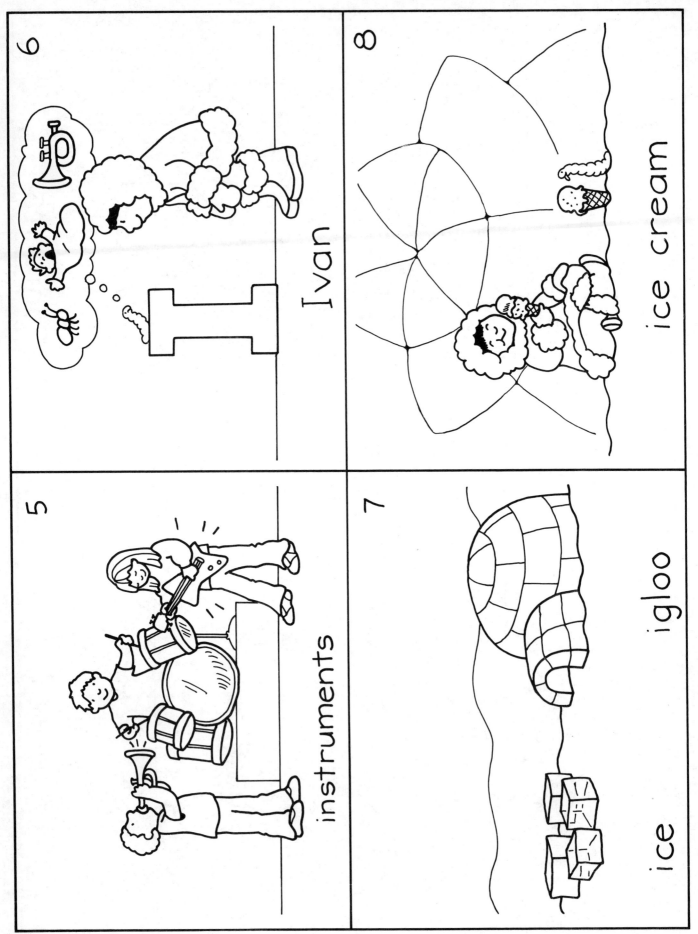

6

I

Ivan

5

instruments

8

ice cream

7

igloo

ice

I am Jolly Jogger.

JOLLY JOGGER

1. Far away, in a jungle jumping with animals, lived Jolly Jogger. Jolly was one of the fastest joggers in all the land. She jogged through the jungle many times each day.

2. Jolly always wore a jacket when she jogged. She liked to collect junk from the jungle and put it in her jacket pockets.

3. Jolly liked to juggle too. She could juggle her junk and jog at the same time. The jungle creatures loved to see her jogging by and juggling.

4. One day while Jolly was jogging in the jungle, she heard something: "J-J-J-J-J-J." What could it be? The sound became louder and louder as she jogged along: "J-J-J-J-J-J!"   (*Have the children make this* **J** *sound with you as the story progresses.*)   She seemed to be getting closer and closer to the sound. Finally she saw an old deserted jeep. The sound was coming from there! "J-J-J-J-J-J!"

5. Jolly peeked inside the jeep and saw a jaguar! He was trapped inside and could not free himself. He looked so frightened and helpless. As he squirmed around, he made this sound: "J-J-J-J-J-J." Jolly said to the jaguar, "Just a minute, Mr. Jaguar, I'll get you out!"

6. Jolly jiggled, jerked, and jumped and jiggled, jerked, and jumped some more on the old jeep. She loosened the jaguar from its trap. You could see the joy in the jaguar's eyes. He was so happy to be free again!

7. Jolly and the jaguar jogged along together through the jungle. Jolly told the jaguar jokes while she impressed him with her juggling.

8. When Jolly and the jaguar got to Jolly's house, they drank juice from a jug. The jaguar thanked Jolly and jumped into the jungle.

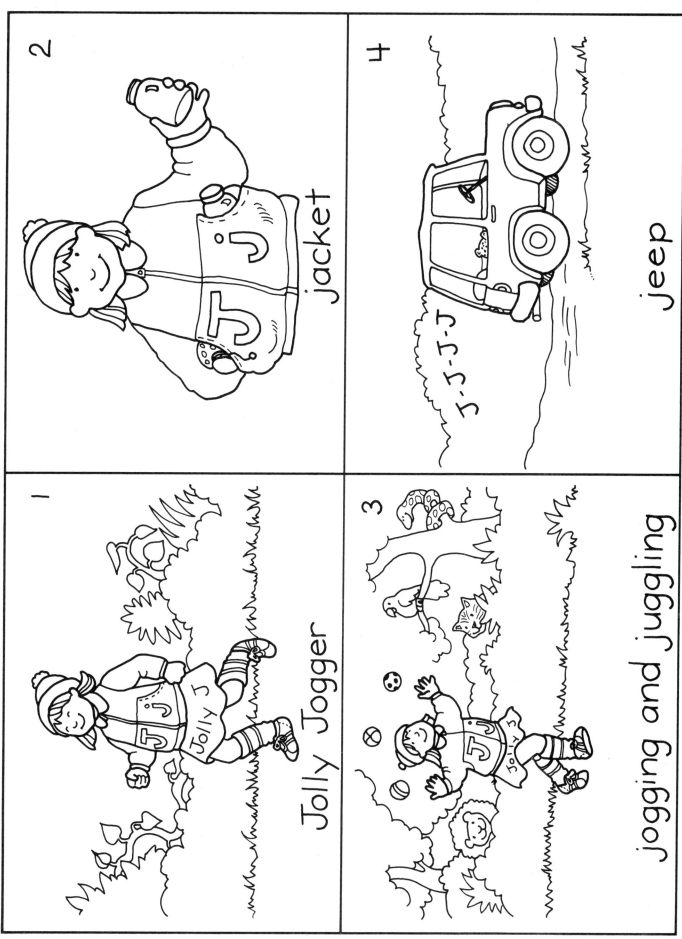

2

jacket

4

j-j-j-j

jeep

1

Jolly Jogger

3

jogging and juggling

41

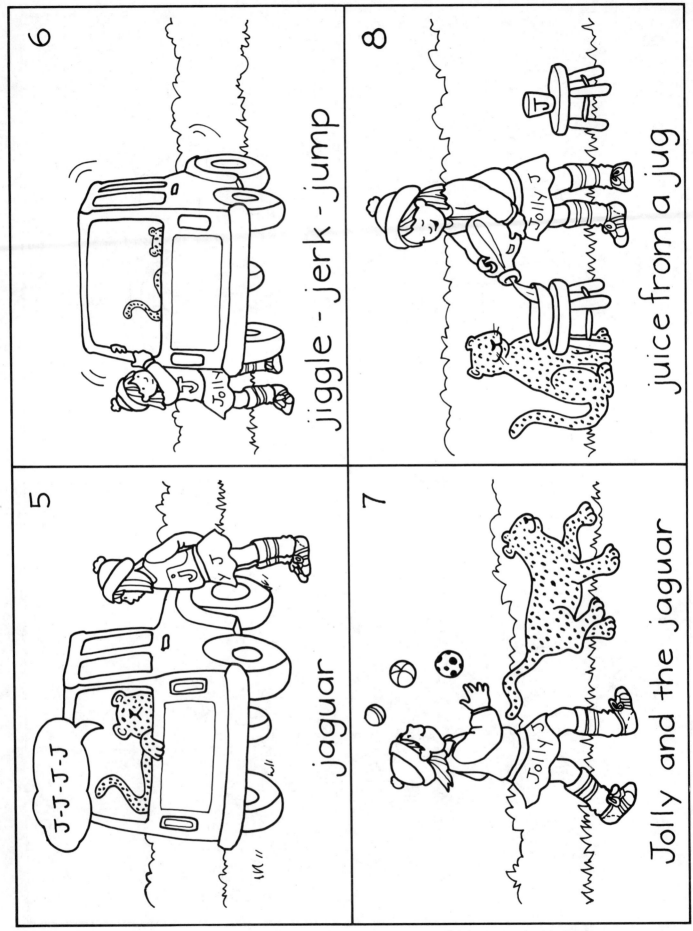

6

jiggle - jerk - jump

8

juice from a jug

5

jaguar

J-J-J-J

7

Jolly and the jaguar

I am Kicky Kangaroo.

KICKY KANGAROO

1. Once upon a time there was a kind kangaroo named Kicky. She was named Kicky because she loved to kick.

2. She carried her baby, Kooky, in her pouch with her wherever she went.

3. One day while Kicky was looking for new things to kick, she found a set of keys. There were four colorful, shiny keys. She put all of them into her pouch with Kooky, then looked about for what the keys might open.

4. Kicky and Kooky came close to a building they had never seen before. The lock on the door was painted bright red, just like one of the keys Kicky had found. She tried the red key in the lock. The key turned, the door opened, and inside they discovered a kitchen! Kicky and Kooky made some tea in a kettle in the kitchen and laughed their happy kangaroo laugh; "K-K-K-K-K-K-K!"   (*Have the children make the* **K** *sound with you as the kangaroos laugh throughout the story.*)

5. Next Kicky took out the blue key. She and Kooky looked around until they found a blue lock. Kicky opened the door to find a kite collection! Every color and kind of kite in the world was there. Kicky and Kooky laughed with joy to see all those kites: "K-K-K-K-K-K-K-K-K!"

6. Then Kicky took out the yellow key. She wondered what it would open. Kooky pointed to a yellow lock on another building. Behind the door with the yellow lock, Kicky and Kooky found a kennel! They visited with the animals for awhile and then went on their way laughing, "K-K-K-K-K-K-K-K!"

7. The last key was green. They looked for a long time for a green lock. They finally saw one on a very large building. When they opened the door, they discovered a kindergarten full of kids! What fun they had together!

8. When the bell rang, the kids got ready to go home. Kicky and Kooky gave each kid a kiss and hopped away, waving and laughing, "K-K-K-K-K-K-K!"

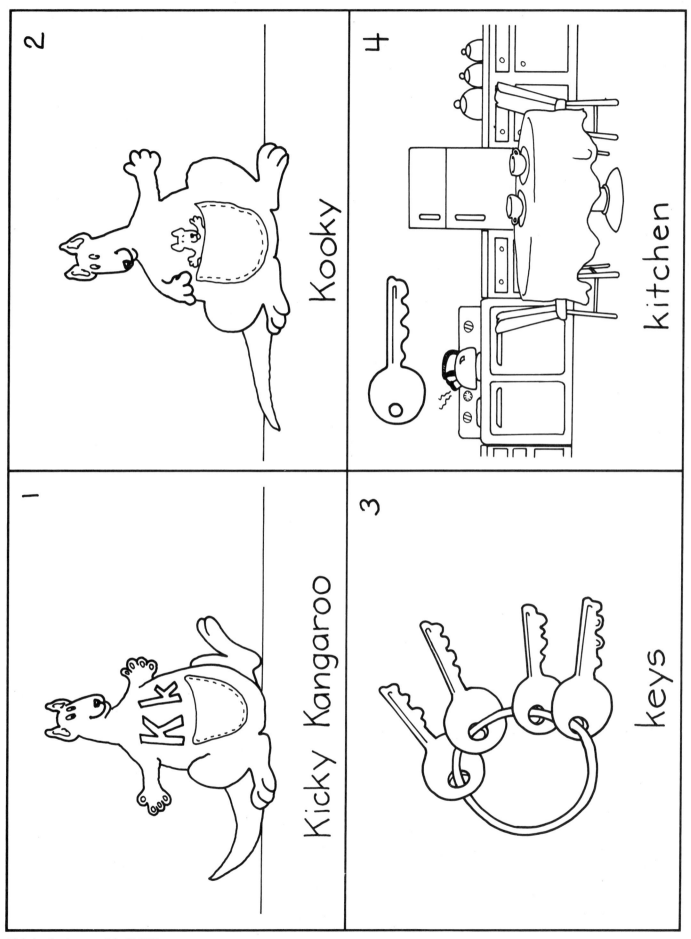

1

Kicky Kangaroo

2

Kooky

3

keys

4

kitchen

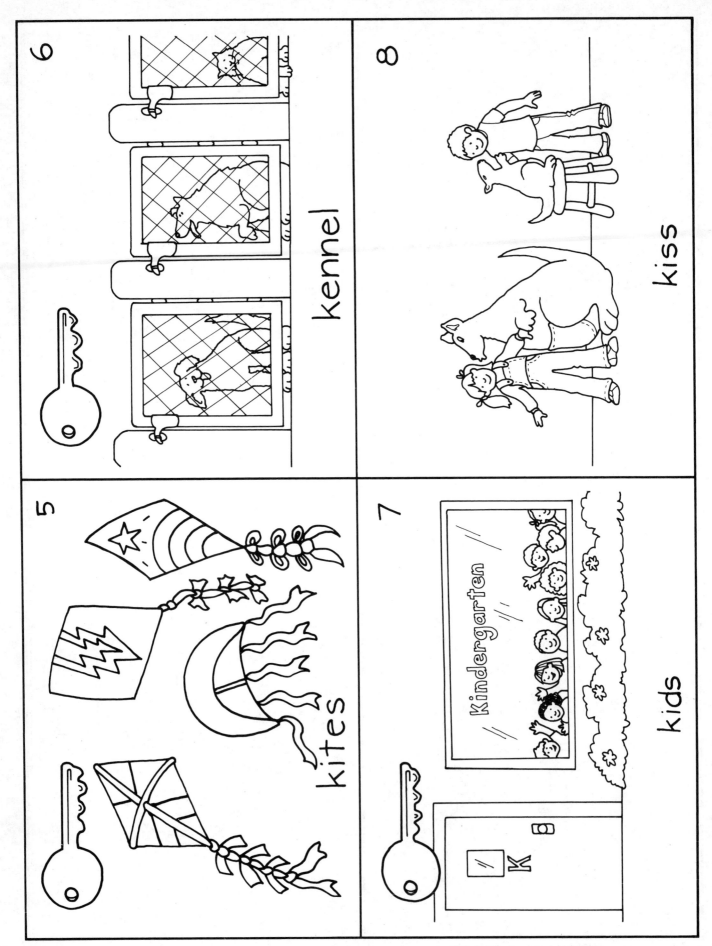

6

kennel

5

kites

8

kiss

7

kids

I am Looney Lion.

LOONEY LION

1. This is the story of Looney Lion. Looney loved to laugh and look at lovely things. He collected leaves from all over Lion Land.

2. One day after lunch, Looney went for a walk by a lake to look for leaves. He was lucky because he found lots and lots of lovely leaves. He could hardly hold all of them. He was trying to arrange them when he looked up and saw a light high in the top of a lemon tree. Leading up to the light was a long, long ladder made of logs. Looney wanted to learn what was up there.

3. Looney put down his leaves under a lemon so they would not blow away. He began leaping up the ladder. When he got part of the way up, he looked and saw a little LIZARD! Looney was frightened and screamed, "Look!" Then he scooted down the ladder: "L-L-L-L-L-L-L-L-L." *(Make the* L *sound with the children singing high and then going down the scale as Looney goes down the ladder. Repeat throughout the story.)* Looney was not brave like other lions.

4. The lizard crawled away, so Looney decided to try again. Up, up, up he went on the long, long ladder. He was higher than the first time when he saw a large LOBSTER! "Look!" he screamed, and scampered down the ladder again: "L-L-L-L-L-L-L-L-L."

5. After the lobster had gone, Looney started up the ladder again. He was most curious to see what was at the top of the lemon tree. This time he was almost to the top when he saw a LEOPARD! "Look!" he screeched, and ran down the ladder: "L-L-L-L-L-L-L-L."

6. Then a line of ladybugs crawled past Looney and went up the ladder. They looked as though they knew what they were doing. Looney decided to follow them and really make it to the top. What could be up there to interest a lizard, a lobster, a leopard, and ladybugs? He was going to find out!

7. This time Looney did make it to the top of the ladder and into the lemon tree. Do you know what he saw? A library! A lady called a librarian was there helping everyone find books. She came over to Looney and asked him if he liked books. She explained that a library was for those who like to read and look at books.

8. Looney learned all about the tree-house library. He checked out some books about lions, lambs, and llamas. Then he went down the ladder lightly and happily: "L-L-L-L-L-L-L-L."

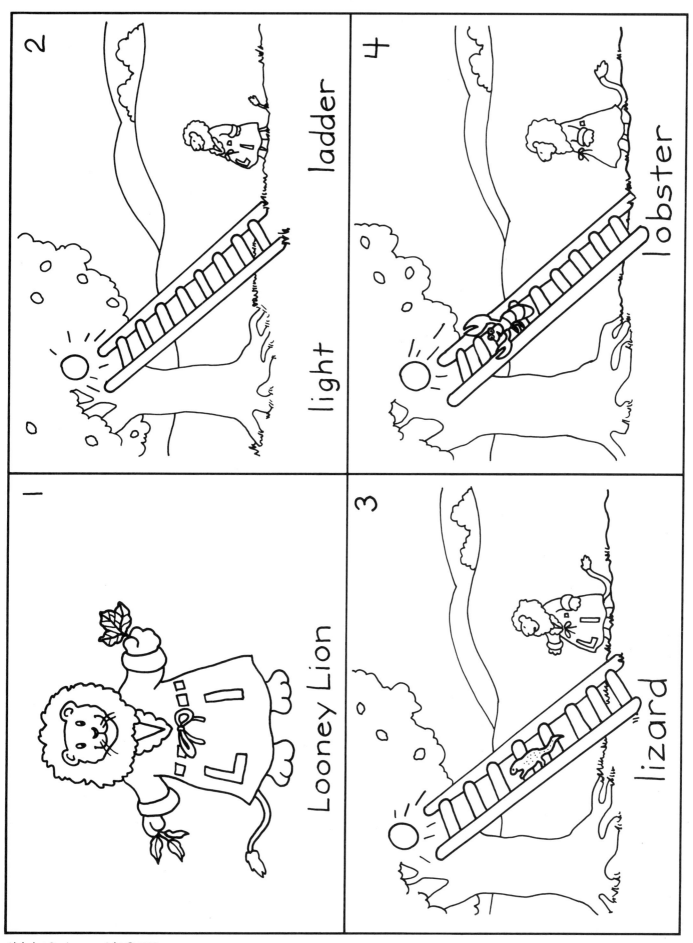

2

light   ladder

1

Looney Lion

4

lobster

3

lizard

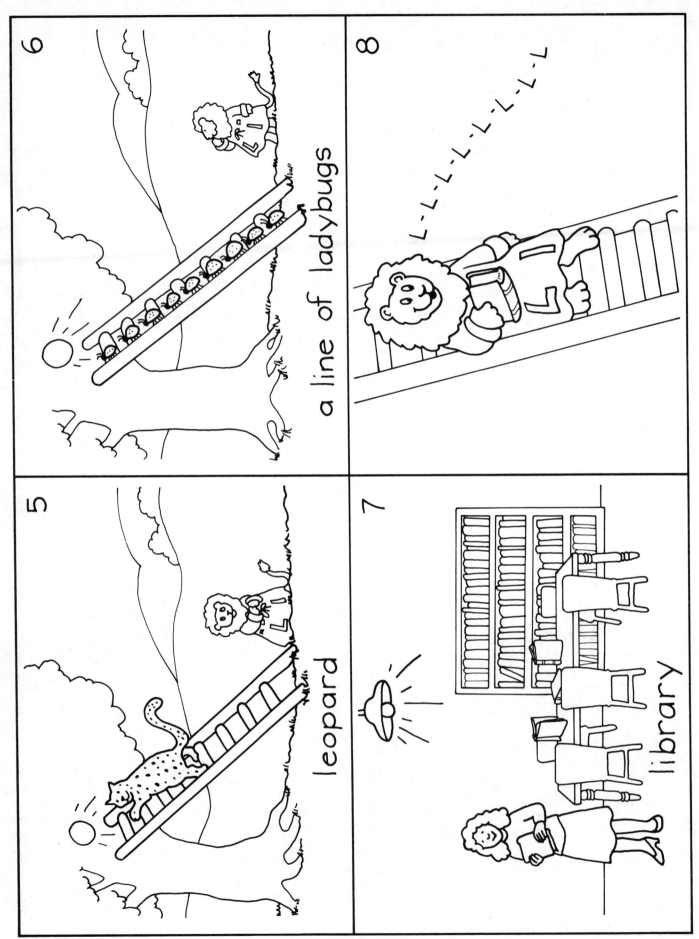

6

a line of ladybugs

5

leopard

8

L-L-L-L-L-L-L

7

library

I am Merry Mouse.

MERRY MOUSE

1. Once upon a time there was a mouse named Merry. Merry lived with Mama Mouse in a mushroom patch on Monster Mountain.

2. Merry and Mama were mail mice. They delivered mail to each mouse hole on Monster Mountain. Sometimes they had mail for Mr. Monster, who lived at the very top of the mountain.

3. One Monday morning, Merry woke up to find marks all over his body—red, scratchy, uncomfortable marks! What was the matter with Merry? Mama Mouse had never see marks like these. Merry felt miserable!

4. Merry and Mama decided to climb Monster Mountain to see Mr. Monster. He was kind and wise and could solve anyone's problems. Since it was a mile to the top of the mountain, Mama and Merry rested in the middle.

5. "My, my," said Mr. Monster as he rubbed his mustache and looked Merry over. "M-M-M-M-M . . . ," he said as he checked Merry's marks.   (*Make the sound of the letter* **M**. *Have the children make it with you.*)   Mr. Monster finally said, "Merry, you have the measles!"

6. Mr. Monster mixed some medicine for Merry to take until the marks disappeared. He also gave Merry special mittens to wear to keep from scratching. The mittens had **M**s on them. He told Merry to get lots of rest until Monday morning came again. Mama and Merry thanked Mr. Monster and went back down the mountain to get Merry well again. Mama delivered the mail alone each day while Merry rested.

7. When Monday morning came again, Merry looked in the mirror and saw that his marks were gone. He called, "Mama, Mama, my marks are missing!"

8. To thank Mr. Monster for making Merry well, Mama and Merry made muffins and took them up the mountain to him. As they munched on the muffins, they all said, "M-M-M-M-M-M!"

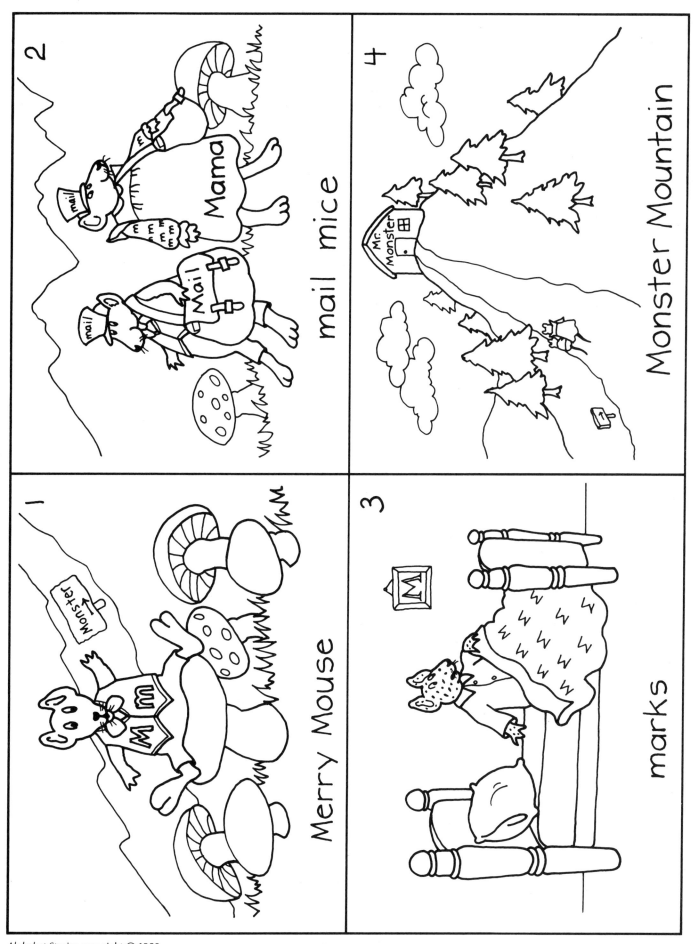

2

Mama

Mail

mail mice

1

Monster

Merry Mouse

4

Mr. Monster

Monster Mountain

3

M

marks

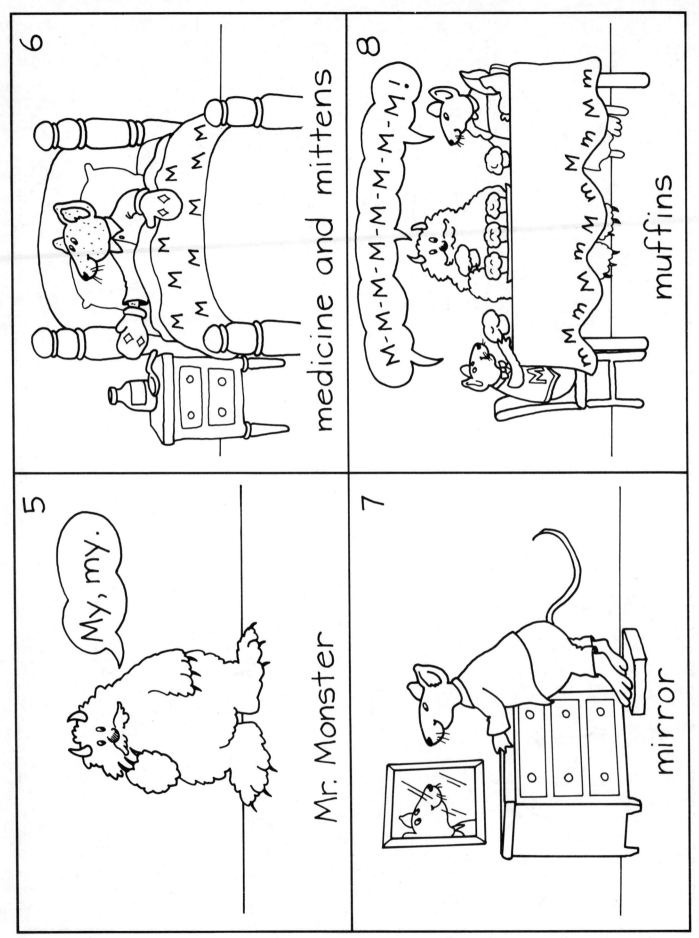

6

medicine and mittens

8

M-M-M-M-M-M!

muffins

5

My, my.

Mr. Monster

7

mirror

I am Noisy Newt.

NOISY NEWT

1. Nestled in a nice nest in Nevada is a newt named Noisy. Noisy is always making noise.

2. Noisy lives in a nest with eight other newts. They are all noisy, but Noisy is the noisiest newt of all. The nine newts sit in their nest night and day and noisily make this sound: "N-N-N-N-N-N-N!"
   (*Have the children make the* **N** *sound throughout the story.*)

3. Noisy and the other newts love the number nine. They often sing "nine" nine times like this: "Nine-nine-nine-nine-nine-nine-nine-nine-nine!" Can you do that?

4. The newts eat nuts and noodles. They leave their nests to look for them. Then they bring the nuts and noodles back to their nests to nibble.

5. One day, when the nine newts were out hunting for nuts and noodles, a nosy porcupine passed by. He tromped right through Noisy's nest and accidentally left a few of his prickly needles. Oh, no! Noisy won't know there are needles in his nest!

6. As night fell, Noisy was the first newt to return to his nest. He crawled into his nice neat nest, got ready to nibble, and shouted, "Oh, no! Needles in my nest!"

7. The other newts heard him and rushed to help. They carried him to see Nifty Nurse. Nifty Nurse carefully pulled all the needles out of Noisy and helped him feel nice again. The other newts were so glad to see that Noisy was OK, they happily made their newt sound: "N-N-N-N-N-N-N!"

8. Noisy thanked Nifty Nurse and went home to what used to be his nice neat nest. He and the other newts took out the nasty needles and said, "No needles now!" From that night on, all the newts carefully checked their nests before crawling in. Can you hear the newts nibbling noisily on their nuts and noodles?
   "N-N-N-N-N-N-N!"

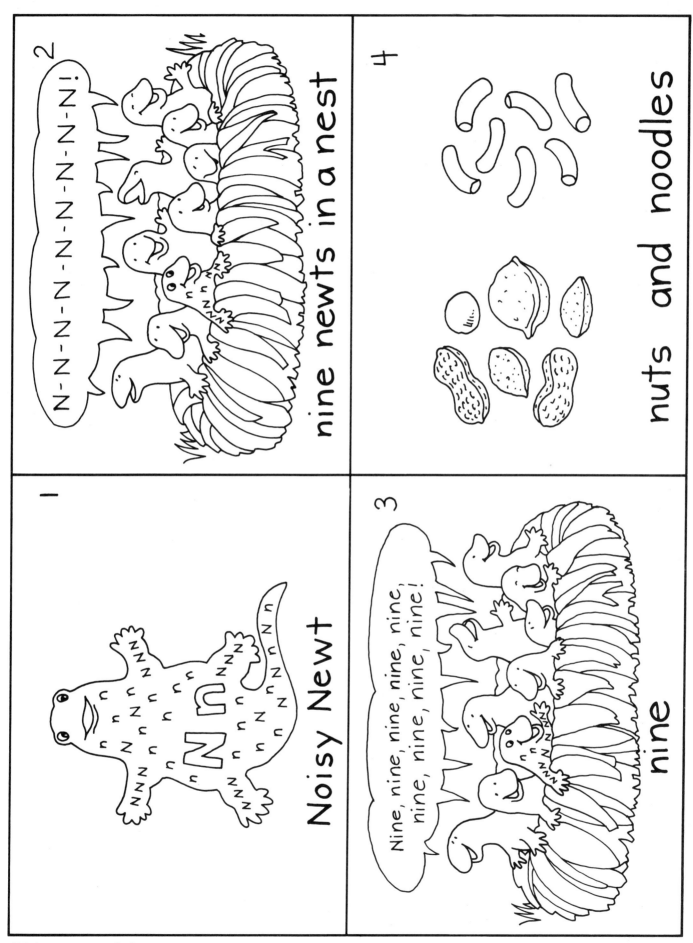

2

N-N-N-N-N-N-N!

nine newts in a nest

4

nuts and noodles

1

Noisy Newt

3

Nine, nine, nine, nine, nine, nine, nine!

nine

no needles now

needles

Nifty Nurse

I am Oh-Oh Octopus.

Alphabet Stories copyright © 1983

59

OH-OH OCTOPUS

1. Once upon a time an octopus named Oh-Oh lived in the ocean.

2. Oh-Oh liked to look for odd objects in the ocean. He had a large collection of them in his office.

3. One day while Oh-Oh was looking for objects, he spotted a box of orange balls. He said, "O-ŏ-ŏ-ŏ!" *(Have the children repeat the short **o** sound with you when it appears in the story.)* "What odd objects! I wonder what they are." He decided to try to find out.

4. Oh-Oh went to see his friend the otter. He asked the otter to come see the box. All the otter could say when he saw the orange balls was, "O-ŏ-ŏ-ŏ! They're odd objects, but I don't know what they are."

5. Oh-Oh and the otter went to find their friend the ostrich. They took the box with them. They called, "Ostrich, ostrich, come out and see our objects!" The ostrich came out and looked. "O-ŏ-ŏ-ŏ!" he said. "What are those odd objects?"

6. Oh-Oh, the otter, and the ostrich next went to see their friend the ox. "Ox, ox," they called, "come and see our objects!" "O-ŏ-ŏ-ŏ! How odd! What are they?" asked the ox. While they were trying to decide how to find out what the orange balls were, an owl flew over. "Let's go ask the owl," they all called out at once.

7. So Oh-Oh, the otter, the ostrich, and the ox went to see the owl. The owl said, "O-ŏ-ŏ-ŏ! You have found some very special objects this time, Oh-Oh." "What are they? What are they?" asked all the animals. The owl explained that they were called oranges and that they were a delicious fruit to eat.

8. Oh-Oh shared the oranges with his friends. *(Have the children name the animals in the story: the otter, the ostrich, the ox, and the owl.)* Everyone said, "O-ŏ-ŏ-ŏ! These oranges are delicious!"

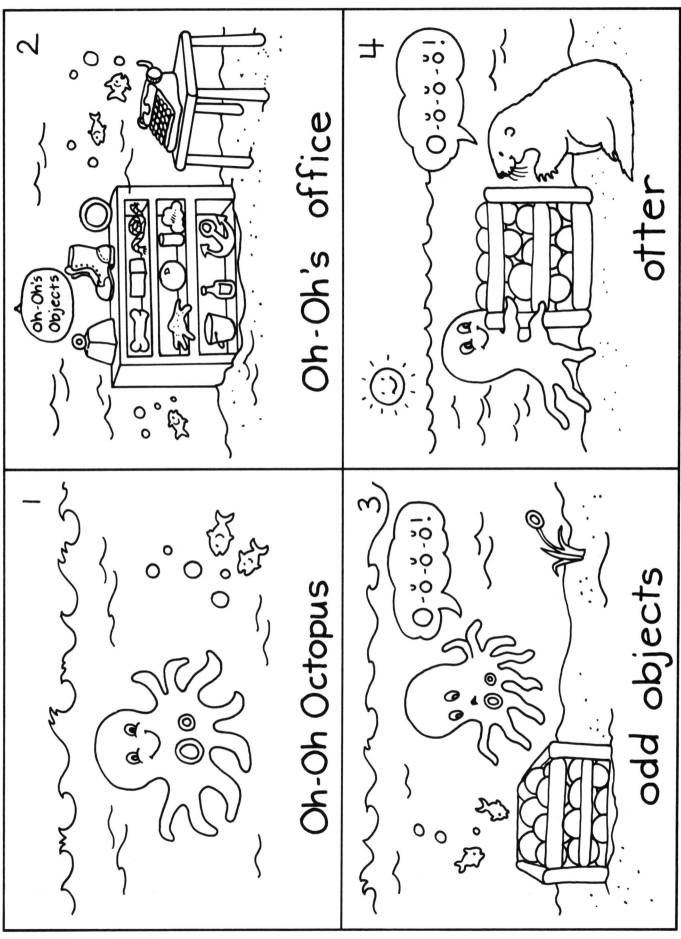

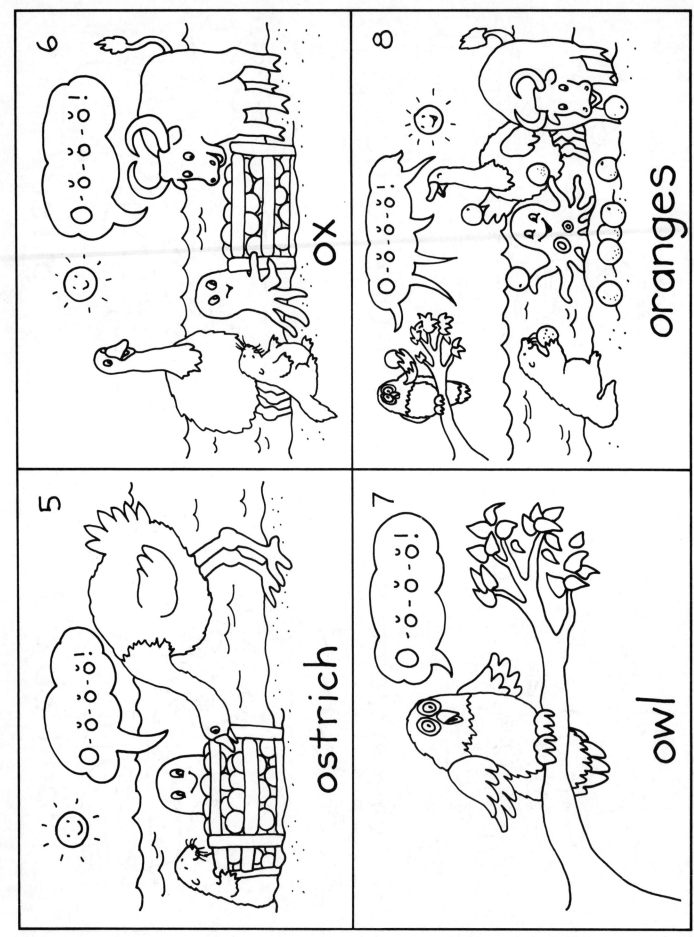

6

ox

5

ostrich

8

oranges

7

owl

I am Polka Pig.

POLKA PIG

1. Once upon a time there was a pretty pig named Polka. She was pink and purple and polka-dotted. She wore a peace sign, a petunia, and a picture of a pumpkin, and she carried a pine cone and a pom-pom wherever she went. Polka loved to go flying and then jump from the plane with her parachute.

2. Polka went up in a plane with her parachute. Pete the Pilot flew the plane. They both ate pickles while they looked for a pretty place to jump with the parachute. When they found a pleasant place, Polka pulled on her parachute. Pete gave Polka a push, and she jumped. After she was out of the way of the plane, she popped open her parachute by pulling a string. Polka's parachute made this sound when it opened: "**P!**"   (*Have the children make the sound of* **P** *with you each time Polka's parachute opens.*)

3. But Polka landed right in a pile of . . . paste! She was all sticky—and not a bit pleased. When Pete picked her up, she told him to be more careful about where he pushed her the next time.

4. The second time Polka flew in the plane with Pete, they ate more pickles while picking out a place to land. When they found a place, Pete gave her a push, and out she went. Polka pulled her parachute string—"**P!**"—and landed right in . . . prickly pine needles! Polka was all prickly and sticky—and not a pit pleased.

5. The third time she flew in Pete's plane, she watched him closely as they ate their pickles. Pete didn't even give Polka time to think before he pushed her out. She pulled the parachute string—"**P!**"—and slowly drifted down into a . . . pool of purple paint! Polka was all painted, prickly, and sticky—and not a bit pleased. When she saw Pete, she told him he was no longer her pilot.

6. Polka went home, cleaned up, and went to bed. She just wanted to forget the plane, the parachute, and Pete. She wanted to forget the paste, the prickly pine needles, and the purple paint.   (*Have the children help recall these things.*)   Polka slept and had a lovely dream about a princess named Penny.

7. Penny gave Polka a magic puffball in the dream. She told Polka always to take it parachuting with her—if she did, she would land only in pleasant places. When Polka woke up, can you guess what was in her hand? A puffball!

8. Polka ran out and found Pete the Pilot. Polka told him he could be her pilot after all. So up they went and down came Polka—"**P!**"— on a pile of pillows, in playgrounds, in pansy patches, on pretty paths, and in many other pleasant places—thanks to Princess Penny and the puffball!

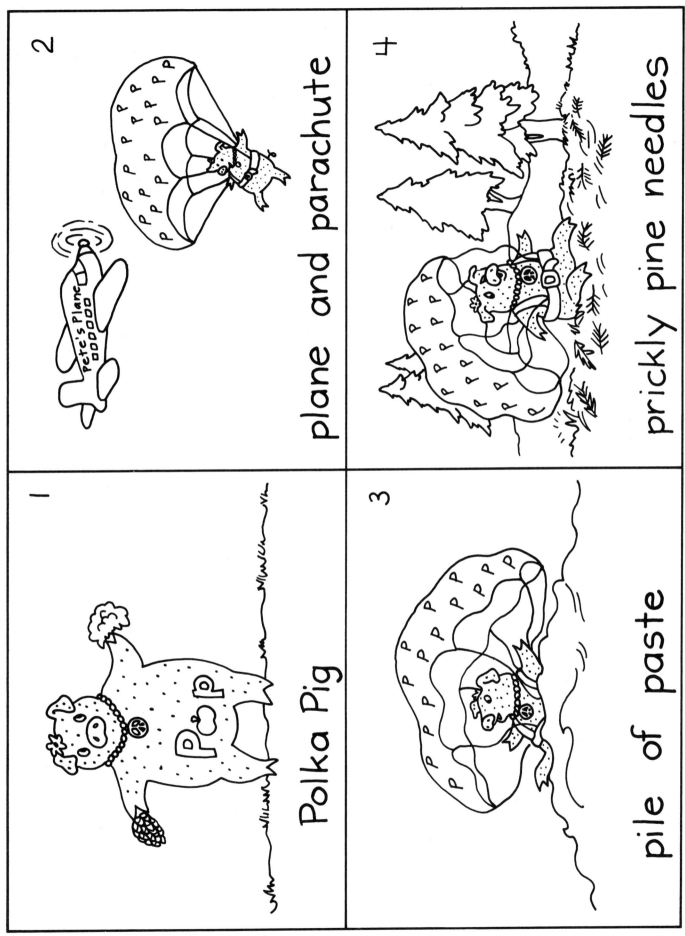

2

plane and parachute

4

prickly pine needles

1

Polka Pig

3

pile of paste

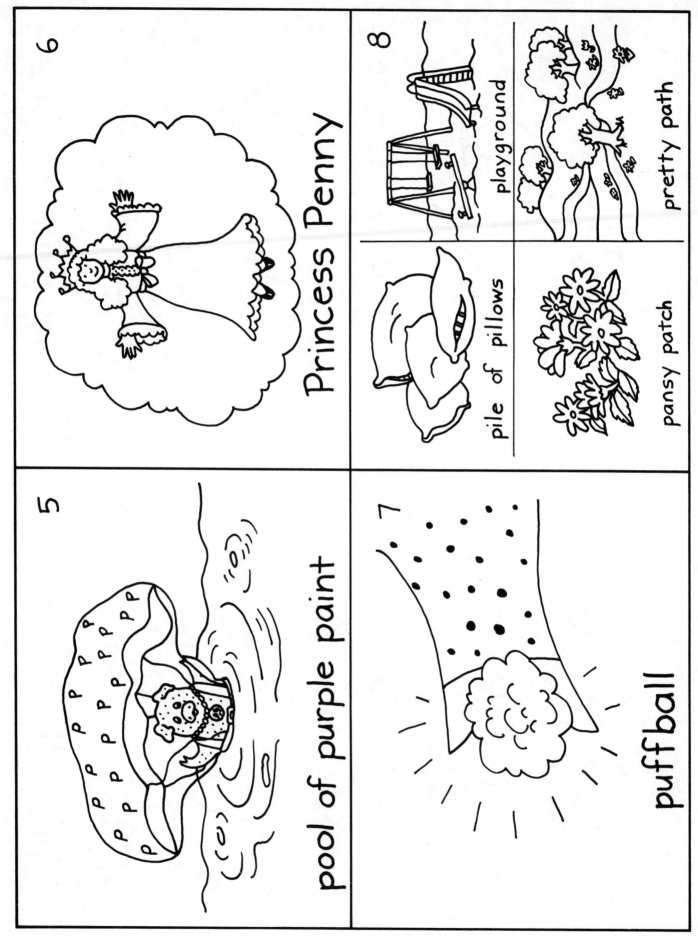

6

Princess Penny

8

playground

pretty path

pile of pillows

pansy patch

5

pool of purple paint

7

puffball

I am Quacky Quacker.

QUACKY QUACKER

1. Once upon a time there was a quacker named Quacky. Quacky loved to quack all the time. She would say, "Qu-qu-quack! Qu-qu-quack!"   (*Have children repeat the quack sound throughout the story.*)

2. Quacky lived on a farm full of quackers. They all loved to quack just like Quacky. They were NEVER quiet.

3. A quarterback came to stay at the Quacker Farm because he needed a quiet, peaceful rest. He heard enough noise from people when he played football as a quarterback. Now he wanted to get some quiet at Quacker Farm.

4. He would yell, "Quiet! Quiet! Quit quacking!" But the quackers would not quit quacking. They'd go, "Qu-qu-quack! Qu-qu-quack!"

5. One day while the quarterback was yelling at the quackers, a queen passed by on the road. She heard the quarterback quarreling with the quackers. She offered to help the quarterback with the quacking problem.

6. She reached into the back of her carriage and produced a "quiet quilt." She explained to the quarterback that if this quilt were hung where the quackers could see it, they would quickly become quiet and remain that way until the quilt was removed. She said it would stop the quacking. The queen held the quilt up in front of the quackers. They quit quacking and were quiet! She took it down and they quacked: "Qu-qu-quack!"

7. The quarterback tried it. The quackers were quiet again. The quarterback thought how nice it was to have quiet quackers. Now he could get some rest.

8. To show the queen his appreciation, he gave her a shiny new quarter. He thanked her and said, "That is quite a quilt!"

2

- Qu-qu-quack! - Qu-qu-quack!

quackers

4

Quiet! Quiet! Quit quacking!

Qq

1

Quacky Quacker

Qq

3

Qq

quarterback

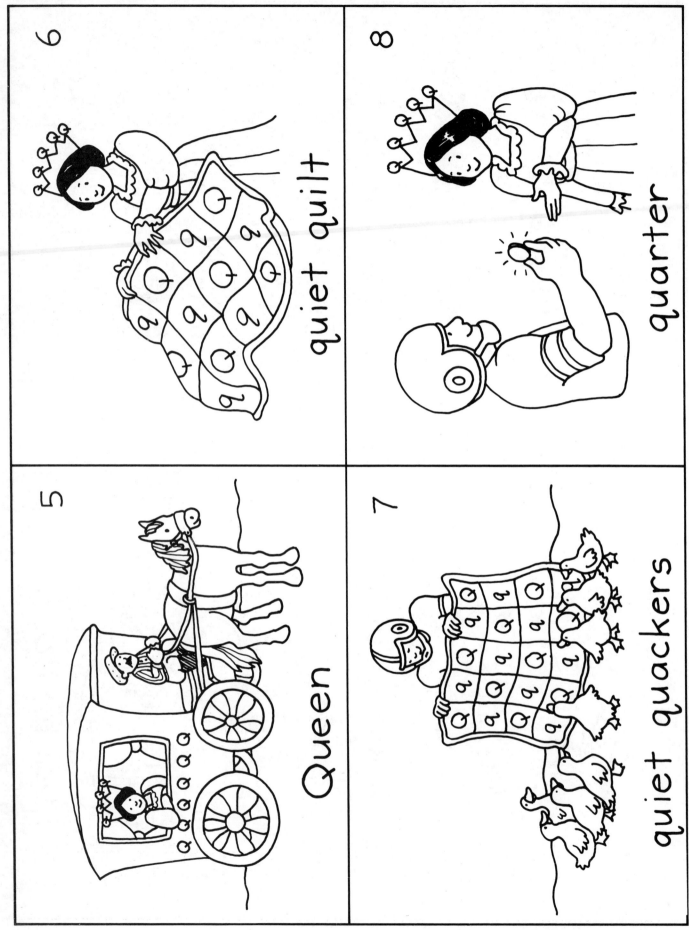

6

quiet quilt

8

quarter

5

Queen

7

quiet quackers

I am Racing Raccoon.

RACING RACCOON

1. Once there was a raccoon named Racing. Racing had rings around his eyes and rosy cheeks, and he always wore rings on a red ribbon around his neck. Racing had won the rings in river races.

2. Racing loved to race down the river on his raft, which was shaped like a rectangle. Racing would row his raft down the rough river. Because he could make it go very fast, he won many river races. Racing's raft made this sound when he paddled with the oar: "R-R-R-R-R-R-R!"   (*Have the children make the sound of* **R** *with you in the story.*)

3. One day, Racing decided to plan a big raft race on the river with all his friends. The animals were all excited, and everyone began to build new rafts for the race.

4. The rabbits made a raft and painted it like a rainbow. They named it "Rainbow Raft." "R-R-R-R-R-R!" went the rainbow raft in the river.

5. The rats made a raft covered with a red rug. They named their raft "Rats' Red Rug Raft." "R-R-R-R-R-R!" went the red rug raft in the water.

6. The reindeer made a raft of rubber. It was round. They named it "Rubber-Runner." "R-R-R-R-R-R!" went this raft in the water.

7. Racing had tied ropes around his raft and named it "Racing's Rope Raft." Now all the rafts were ready for the race on the river.

8. The robins in the trees began the race by chirping out, "Ready, Set, Row!" The water rippled as the racers rowed down the river. "R-R-R-R-R-R-R-R!" went all the rafts.   (*Make the sound loudly this time.*)   Racing reached the finish line first and won another ring for his ribbon. Everyone was happy for him. They shouted, "Rah, rah, rah, Racing Raccoon!"

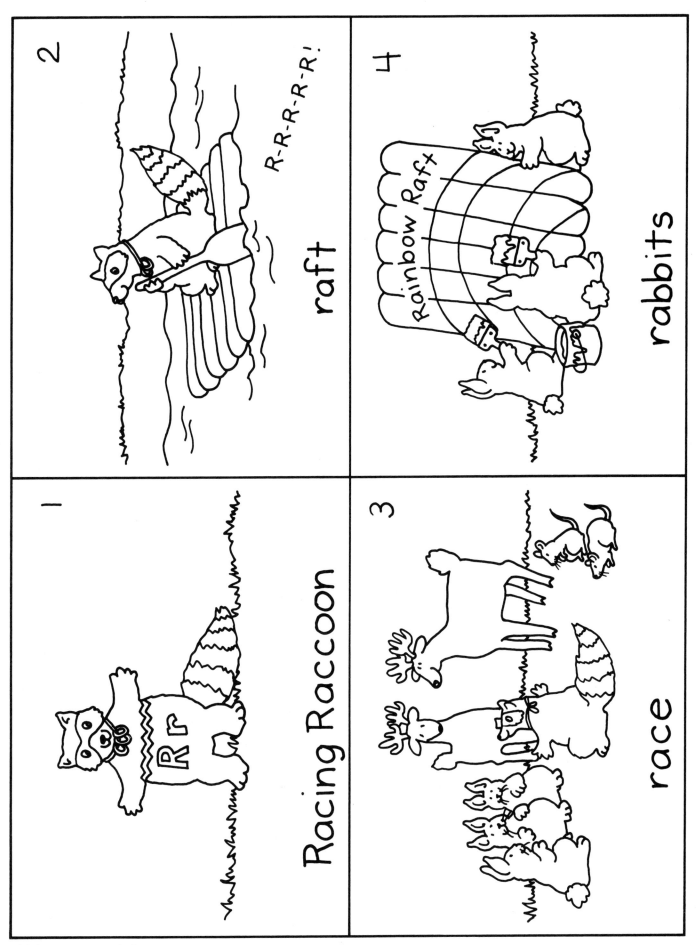

2

raft

R-R-R-R-R!

4

rabbits

Rainbow Raft

1

Racing Raccoon

Rr

3

race

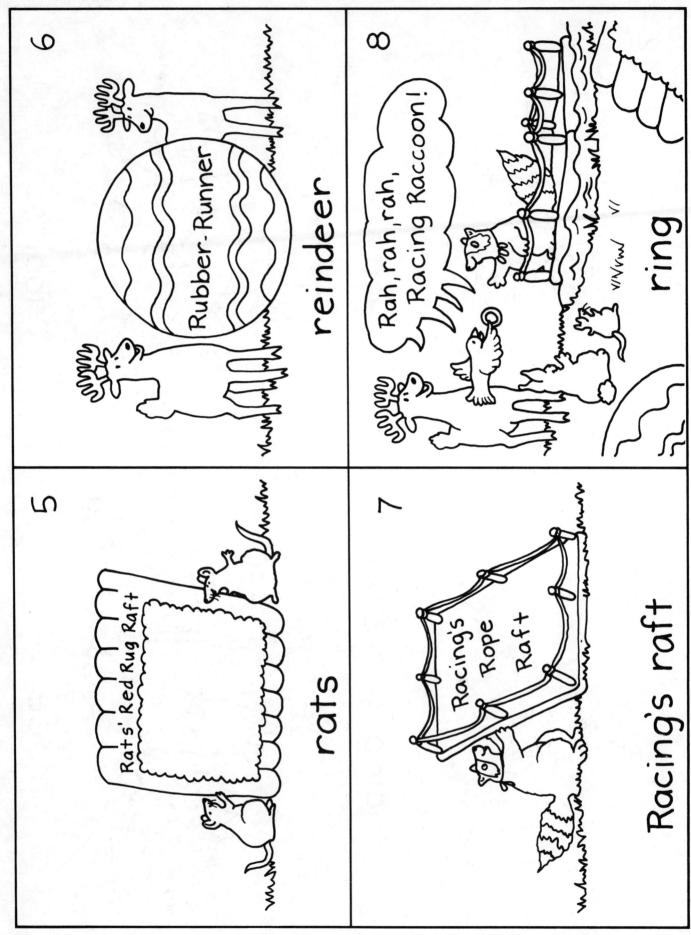

6

Rubber-Runner

reindeer

8

Rah, rah, rah,
Racing Raccoon!

ring

5

Rats' Red Rug Raft

rats

7

Racing's
Rope
Raft

Racing's raft

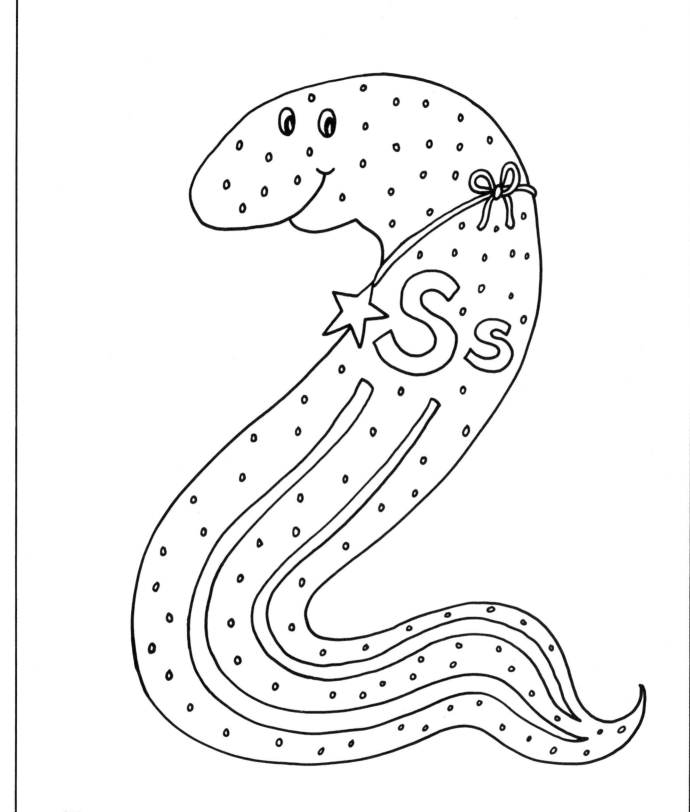

I am Spotty Snake.

SPOTTY SNAKE

1. Slipping and sliding in the sand on the way to Snake Singing School was Spotty Snake. She taught snakes how to sing. She was spotted and striped and always smiling.

2. Spotty always stood on a special stool when it was time for singing. She held a stick that the singing snakes could see. She would swing and sweep her stick as the snakes sang like this: "S-S-S-S-S-S-S-S-S-S-S!" *(Have the children pretend to sing while making the sound of S.)*

3. Spotty always wore a special silver star on a string. Everyone knew she was a special singer by that silver star.

4. One day while Spotty was on her stool swinging her stick, she stretched farther than usual and accidentally did a somersault, falling off the stool. What a scramble as all the snakes came to see if she was OK! Spotty was fine, but her silver star had broken!

5. Spotty felt sick and sad. She slithered away to her home—a submarine sunk at the seaside. There she stayed, too sad to come back to singing school.

6. The snakes felt sorry for their special singing teacher. They planned a secret surprise for her. They went to some stores and looked for stars. They found a beautiful silver star just like the one that had broken. It cost six dollars. For another dollar, they could get a silk string to hang it from. They needed seven dollars.

7. The snakes held a school sale to earn the money. They went home and collected things that they had saved: spools, spoons, stamps, string, socks, seashells, sponges, and stones. They made signs so everyone would know about their sale. The signs said: SUPER SCHOOL SALE! After the sale, they counted their money. One, two, three, four, five, six, seven dollars! They had enough! They slid to the star store and bought the silver star and the silk string. They wrapped up the gift in a spotted sock.

8. The snakes slipped over to the submarine. How surprised Spotty was when the snakes gave her the sock! She was so happy she started to sing, "S-S-S-S-S-S-S-S-S!" She put the new silver star on, thanked the snakes, and sang this song (tune of "Twinkle, Twinkle"):

   > Special special silver star,
   > Stay with me just where you are.
   > Thanks to all my singing friends,
   > Now I'll teach you once again.
   > Special special silver star,
   > Stay with me just where you are!

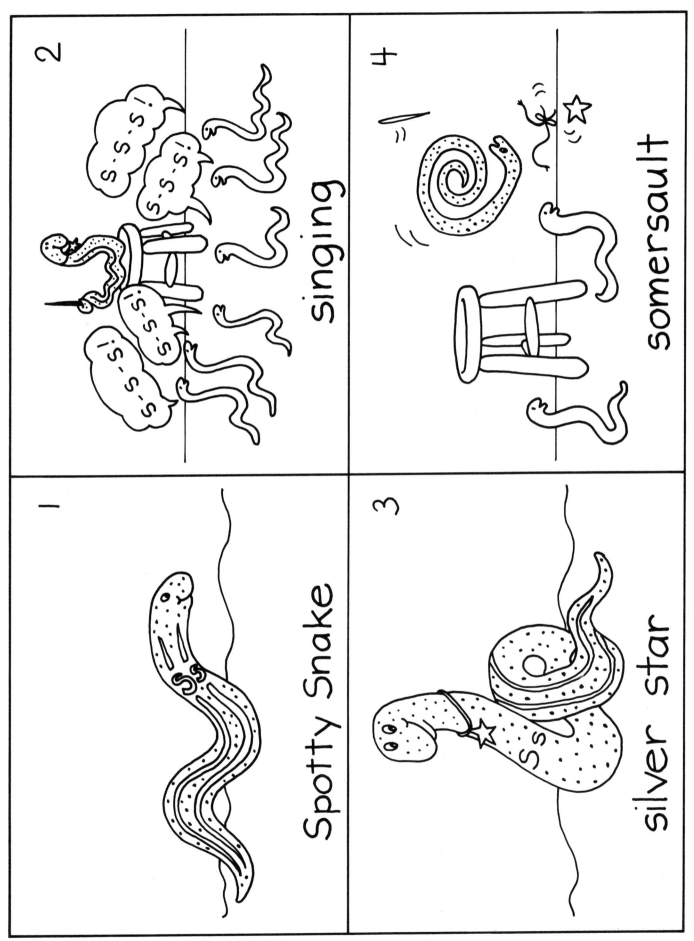

2

s-s-s
s-s-s
S-S-S

singing

4

somersault

1

Spotty Snake

3

silver star

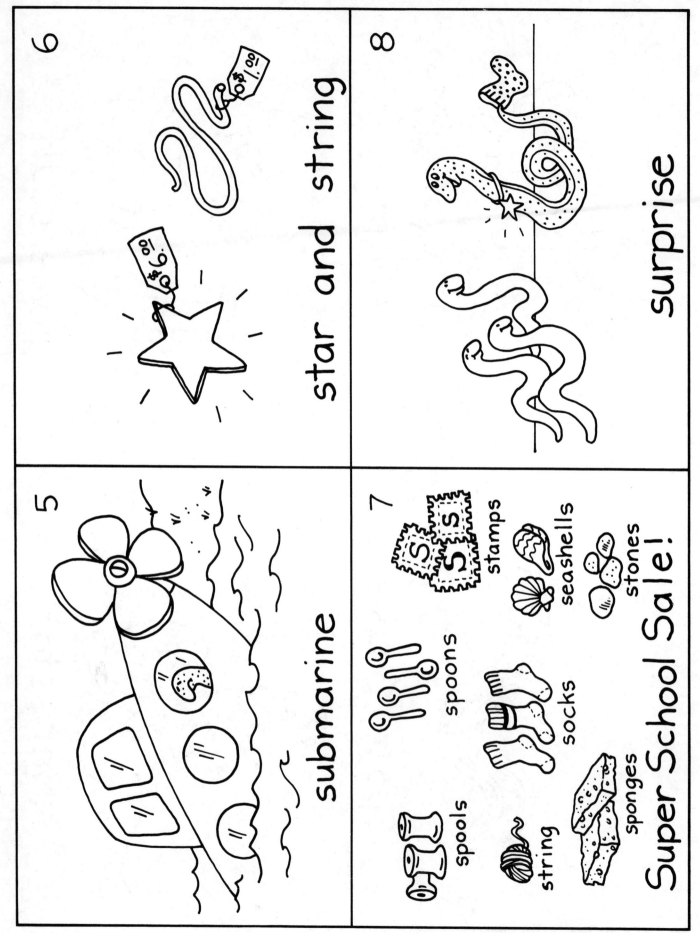

6

star and string

8

surprise

5

submarine

7

stamps

seashells

stones

spoons

socks

spools

string

sponges

Super School Sale!

I am Tricky Turkey.

TRICKY TURKEY

1. Once upon a time there was a turkey named Tricky. Tricky was a tan turkey with ten feathers in her tail, two teeth, and a tongue. She wore a tutu with a tie. She was called "Tricky" because she did all sorts of tricks. She could play a tambourine and dial a telephone with her toes, and she could tumble. Imagine, a tumbling turkey!

2. Many turkeys lived with Tricky on the turkey farm. They liked to play tag in teams. Sometimes they wore T-shirts so they could keep track of the teams. Tricky's team usually won the games because Tricky knew so many tricks.

3. One Tuesday, a terrible tornado blew through the turkey farm. Everything was tossed, turned, tangled, twisted, and twirled about.

4. When the tornado was over, Tricky found herself on top of an old taxi parked between two trees. She could not see any other turkeys or anyone else, either. She tumbled off the top of the taxi, hopped inside, and use some tricks to get it started.

5. Tricky drove the taxi with her two toes! She took a tour of the area to see if anyone needed her help. What was this she saw? Why, it was a tower of turtles! She counted them: "One, two, three, four, five, six, seven, eight, nine, ten!" The tornado must have tossed them like that.

6. Tricky took the turtles down one at a time, starting from the top. They were tired from being tossed in the tornado. Tricky told them to rest while she made a treat.

7. Tricky found a table, a tablecloth, and some bread. She fixed tasty toast and tea for the turtles. Now the turtles needed a new home to sleep in. Tricky looked and looked.

8. At last Tricky and the turtles found an old tent. The turtles tiptoed in and quickly fell asleep. Before long, you could hear the turtles snoring.   (*Make the sound of indrawn breath, then T-T-T-T-T-T. Repeat the snore several times, having the children make the sounds with you.*)   Tricky returned to her taxi, drove it back between the two trees, and went to sleep, too.   (*Have the children make the same snoring sounds as for the turtles.*)

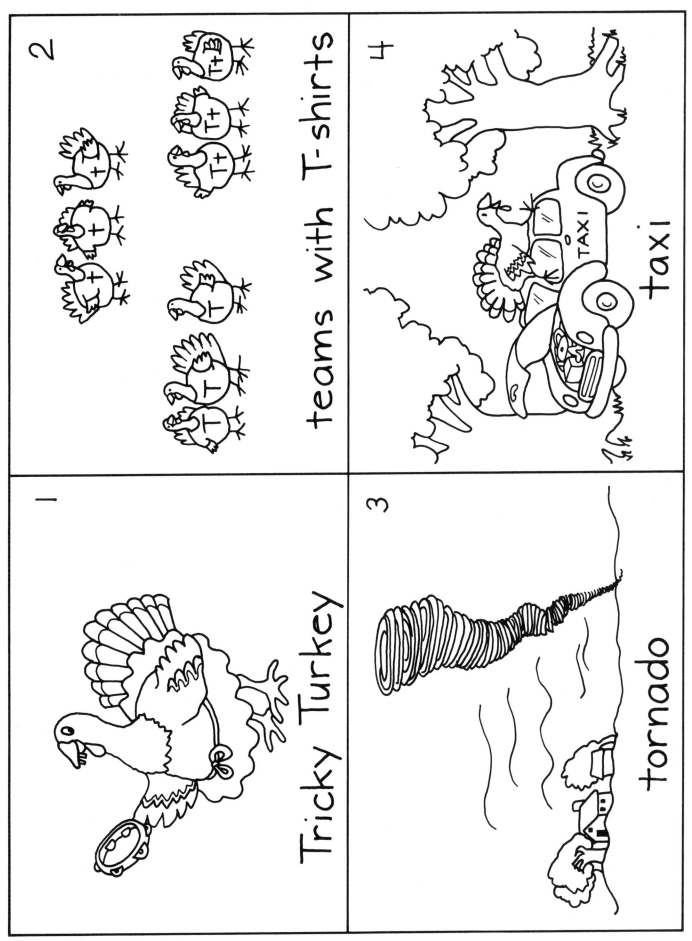

2

teams with T-shirts

4

taxi

1

Tricky Turkey

3

tornado

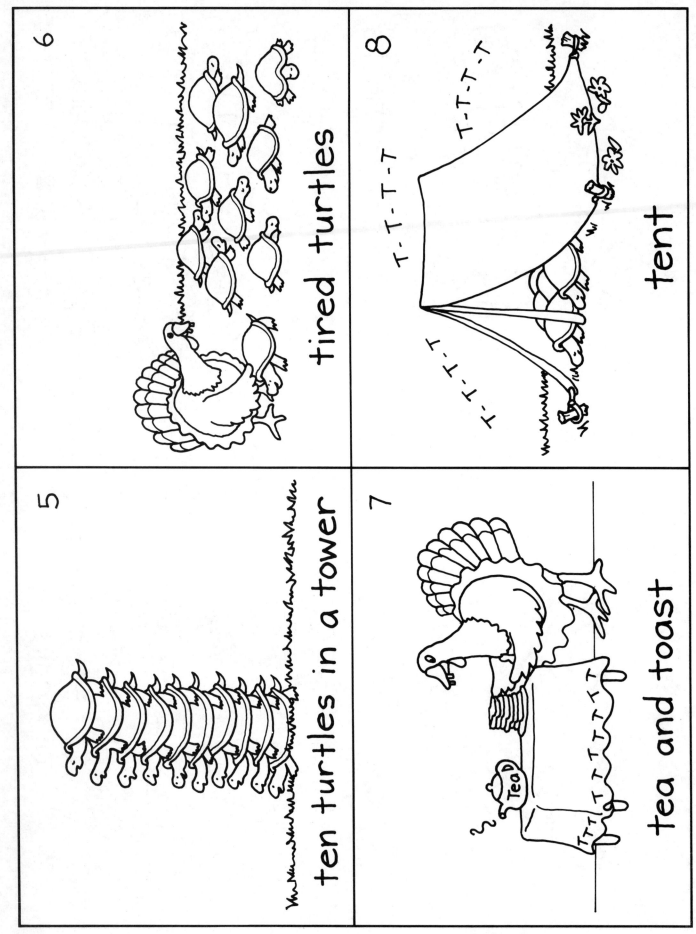

6

tired turtles

8

tent

5

ten turtles in a tower

7

tea and toast

T-T-T-T

T-T-T

T-T-T

T-T-T-T

Tea

I am Ugboo.

UGBOO

1. Far away in the regions of outer space is a planet called UgUgUg. On that planet lived a creature name Ugboo. Ugboo had an unusual magic umbrella that could take him anywhere in the universe. He said these magic words to make it go: "Ug a boo, ug a boo, and a boo boo ug a."

2. Early one morning Ugboo picked up his umbrella and said the magic words, "Ug a boo, ug a boo, and a boo boo ug a." He sailed away to a strange land that was much like a jungle. Being tired, he lay down and fell asleep under a tree with his umbrella next to him. He awakened to an unusual sound: "U-ŭ-ŭ-ŭ-ŭ-ŭ-ŭ-ŭ!" (*Have the children make this sound with you in the story.*) He looked around but saw nothing, so he went back to sleep.

3. Soon he heard the noise again: "U-ŭ-ŭ-ŭ-ŭ-ŭ-ŭ-ŭ!" Ugboo looked around again, but since he saw nothing, he went back to sleep once more. The noise came again, much louder this time: "U-ŭ-ŭ-ŭ-ŭ-ŭ-ŭ!" Then Ugboo saw some little purple creatures peeking at him from behind the tree.

4. "Who are you?" asked Ugboo. They answered, "U-ŭ-ŭ-ŭ-ŭ-ŭ! We are the Uglies. We want your magic umbrella!" Ugboo shook his head and said that he just could not give up his umbrella. He would think of something else they would like instead.

5. Ugboo quickly flew home to UgUgUg and wrapped up an undershirt decorated with **U**s. He showed it to the Uglies when he returned to the jungle. They shook their heads from side to side saying, "Uh-uh. Uh-uh. We want your magic umbrella. Give us your magic umbrella!" Ubgoo said that he would find them something else.

6. Ugboo flew home and returned with his unicycle. He showed it to the Uglies, but they just shook their heads and said, "Uh-uh. Uh-uh. We want your magic umbrella. Give us your magic umbrella!"

7. Ugboo returned home and came back with his ukelele. He asked the Uglies to listen to the lovely sounds it made. But the Uglies shook their heads and said, "Uh-uh. Uh-uh. We want your magic umbrella. Give us your magic umbrella!"

8. Ugboo thought of one last thing the Uglies might want. He hurried home and returned with a large jug. It was filled with a delicious drink called Unpop. He poured some for each Ugly. They tasted it and smiled, shaking their heads up and down this time, and said, "Uh-huh! Uh-huh! We want Unpop! You can keep your umbrella!" So, happily, Ugboo kept his umbrella and brought the Uglies Unpop from time to time.

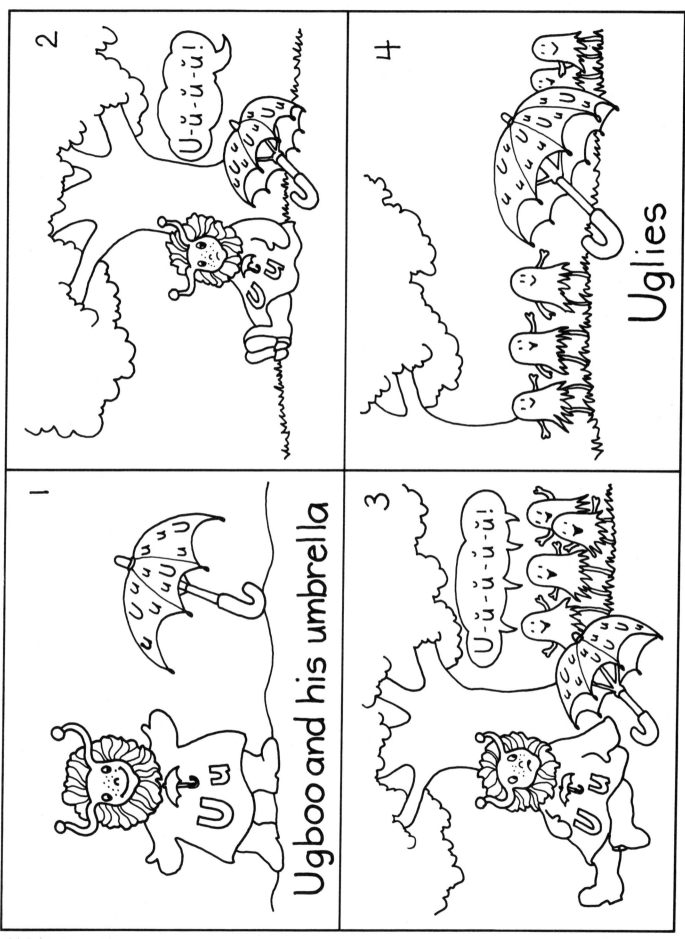

2

ŭ-ŭ-ŭ!

4

Uglies

1

Ugboo and his umbrella

3

ŭ-ŭ-ŭ-ŭ!

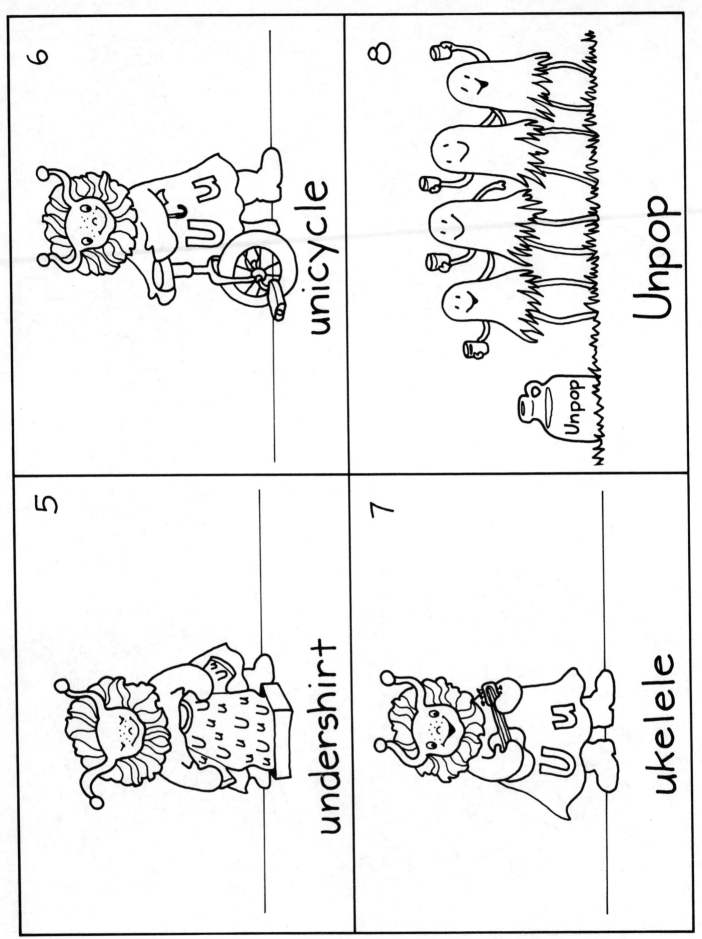

6

unicycle

8

Unpop

5

undershirt

7

ukelele

I am Vam Vampire.

VAM VAMPIRE

1. Once upon a time there was a vampire named Vam. Vam wore a veil so that no one could see how really scary she was. She also wore a vest with her favorite letter on it—**V**. Her fangs were in the shape of **V**s, and so was her nose.

2. Vam had lots of vim, vigor, and vitality because she ate all kinds of vegetables and always took her vitamins. Most vampires drink blood, but not Vam Vampire. She drank vinegar!

3. Vam's favorite thing to do was to vibrate. She shook all over like this: "V-V-V-V-V-V-V-V!"   (*Stand up and wiggle all over making the sound of **V**. Have the children do this with you.*)

4. One day Vam decided to take a vacation. She wanted to visit Valentine Village. She knew many vampires who lived there. She had always wanted a view of a certain valley of violets near the village, too. She packed her valise and got ready to go.

5. Vam turned on her special vacuum—"V-V-V-V-V-V-V-V-V-V-V-V!"— hopped on it and sailed off into the air to find Valentine Village.

6. When she got there, Vam visited all her vampire friends, tried new vegetables, and had a very nice time. She learned to play volleyball and makes vases.

7. Vam made a very nice vase for her friend Vera Vampire and filled it with violets from the valley. She knew that vampires, like anyone else, loved to get flowers. As Vam prepared to leave Valentine Village, she called to her vampire friends, "Good-bye, vampires! Come and visit ME!"

8. Vam climbed onto her vacuum and started it up again: "V-V-V-V-V-V-V-V-V!" She flew back to her own vampire village. There she stopped at the home of Vera Vampire to give her the vase with violets from Valentine Village's valley.

2

Vitamin

Vinegar

vegetables, vinegar, and vitamins

4

Valentine Village

Violet Valley

vacation

1

Vam Vampire

3

v-v-v-v
v-v-v-v
v-v-v-v
v-v-v-v
v-v-v-v
v-v-v-v
v-v-v-v
v-v-v-v
v-v-v-v
v-v-v-v

vibrate

6

volleyball and vases

8

Vera Vampire

5

vacuum

7

vase with violets

I am Wacky Walrus.

WACKY WALRUS

1. Once upon a time, deep in the white wilderness of Wyoming, there lived a woolly walrus named Wacky, who had a wig and whiskers. Her name was Wacky because she did wacky, silly things like waltzing and wiggling. Have you ever heard of a walrus doing that?

2. Wacky lived in a wigwam. The wigwam kept her warm in the winter. She had a little friend name Wiggly Worm. Wacky would pull Wiggly in his little worm wagon, and together they would whistle, whisper, and wink.

3. One day Wiggly Worm decided to play a trick on Wacky. Wiggly wandered away and hid in some weeds. Wacky looked and looked and looked for Wiggly. She called, "Wiggly, where are you?" When Wacky could not find the worm, she sat down and wept, "Wah, wah, wah, wah! Wah, wah, wah, wah!" Finally Wiggly made little sounds—"W-w-w-w-w!"—and Wacky found him in the weeds. (*Have the children weep and make the sound of* **W** *for Wiggly throughout the story.*)

4. Wiggly enjoyed his trick so much that the next day he hid again. This time he hid in a pile of wood. Wacky looked and called, "Wiggly, where are you?" Wacky even looked in the weeds where Wiggly was before, but there was no worm there, "Wah, wah, wah, wah! Wah, wah, wah, wah!" she wept. Soon Wiggly made his little sound from the wood—"W-w-w-w-w-w!"—and Wacky found him again.

5. By now, Wiggly was enjoying all the trouble he was causing. The next day he wiggled away and went into the waves in the water. Wacky looked and looked. She wept again when she couldn't find Wiggly: "Wah, wah, wah, wah! Wah, wah, wah, wah!" Wiggly made his sound from the water—"W-w-w-w-w-w!"—and Wacky discovered where he was.

6. Wacky was weary of Wiggly's tricks and tried to watch him so he would not disappear again. But, being weary, she fell asleep. This time Wiggly wiggled off to an old washing machine. When Wacky could not find him she wept loudly: "Wah, wah, wah, wah! Wah, wah, wah, wah!" Later she heard him in the washing machine: "W-w-w-w-w!" Wacky asked Wiggly, "Why, why, WHY do you wander away?"

7. Wiggly told Wacky that he wanted a wigwam like hers. If he had one, he would never wander away again.

8. So Wacky and Wiggly worked together and made a white, woolly wigwam for Wiggly. Now they are always together. Wiggly never wanders away anymore. Wiggly and Wacky waltz, walk, waddle, whirl, and whistle together all week long.

I am X-Ray X.

95

X-RAY X

1. Once upon a time there was a little creature named X-Ray X. He loved the look of **X** and had a house shaped just like it. Even his nose was in the shape of an **X**, and he had **X**s all over his clothes.

2. X-Ray X was an expert at reading X-rays. He traveled all over the world studying them. He taught doctors and nurses to use them for helping people and animals.

3. One day while X-Ray X was walking down the hall of a building, he heard the shouting of many people. He stopped to see what was happening. X-Ray X liked to help people whenever he could.

4. He stepped into a room and found many confused men and women. They told X-Ray X that they were in charge of naming all the letters of the alphabet. They were all finished except for naming this letter: **X**. X-Ray X was very surprised to find the shape of his nose and his house to be at the bottom of such confusion.

5. He listened to them as they tried out the alphabet with different ideas for that letter. First they tried **gump**. "A B C D E F G H I J K L M N O P Q R S T U V W **GUMP** Y Z." They all shouted, "No, no! That doesn't sound right at all!" Then they tried **slosh**. "A B C D E F G H I J K L M N O P Q R S T U V W **SLOSH** Y Z." They shouted again, "No, no! That doesn't sound right either!"

6. X-Ray X told them about his name and asked them if they would like to try the **X** part for their letter. They tried it: "A B C D E F G H I J K L M N O P Q R S T U V W **X** Y Z." Excitedly they cried, "Wow, that's it! That is the sound we have been listening for!"

7. The people thanked X-Ray X for his letter name and his help. Everyone made **X**s by putting their arms in that shape. X-Ray X said goodbye and went on his way.

8. X-Ray X could hear the people saying the completed alphabet again: "A B C D E F G H I J K L M N O P Q R S T U V W X Y Z." On the letter **X**, they all clapped with joy. Can you do that?

X-rays

X-Ray X

6

8

5

A B C D E F G H
I J K L M N O
P Q R S T U
V W ? Y Z

7

A B C D E F G H
I J K L M N O
P Q R S T U
V W X Y Z !

98

I am Yodeling Yak.

YODELING YAK

1. Once upon a time there lived a young, yellow yak named Yodeling Yak. Yodeling Yak was very good to everyone and always said "Yes! Yes!" when she was asked for help.

2. Yodeling Yak lived in a yak yard with many other young yaks. The yaks liked to eat yams and yogurt. They would yell and yelp while they ate.

3. Yodeling Yak was an expert at yodeling. She would yodel in the yak yard like this: "Yo-da-lay-he-who!" The other yaks would answer, "Yo-da-lay-he-who!"

4. One day while Yodeling Yak was yodeling around in the yak yard, she found a yellow yo-yo. She went over to it and yanked at it. She found that the string went in and out as she pulled on it. She yelled to all the other yaks to come and watch her yanking the yo-yo by its string.

5. Yodeling Yak practiced yanking the yo-yo every day and became very good at making it go up and down. The other yaks watched and yelled, "Y-Y-Y-Y-Y-Y!" each time the yo-yo went up and down. (*Have the children make the sound of* **Y** *with you when the yaks are yelling.*)   "Yea for yo-yos!" yelled the yaks.

6. One day some of the yaks found a poster telling about a yo-yo contest. They brought Yodeling Yak to see it and she decided to enter the yo-yo contest.

7. People of all ages came to try and win the contest with their colorful yo-yos. But there was only one yak: Yodeling Yak. All the people were so good at handling their yo-yos! When it was Yodeling Yak's turn, her yak friends yelled, "Y-Y-Y-Y!" After all the contestants had had their turn, the judges announced the winner: Yodeling Yak! Everyone cheered, "Yea for Yodeling Yak!"

8. The prize was a yacht trip to Yugoslavia. Yodeling Yak brought her yo-yo along and taught others how to use it.

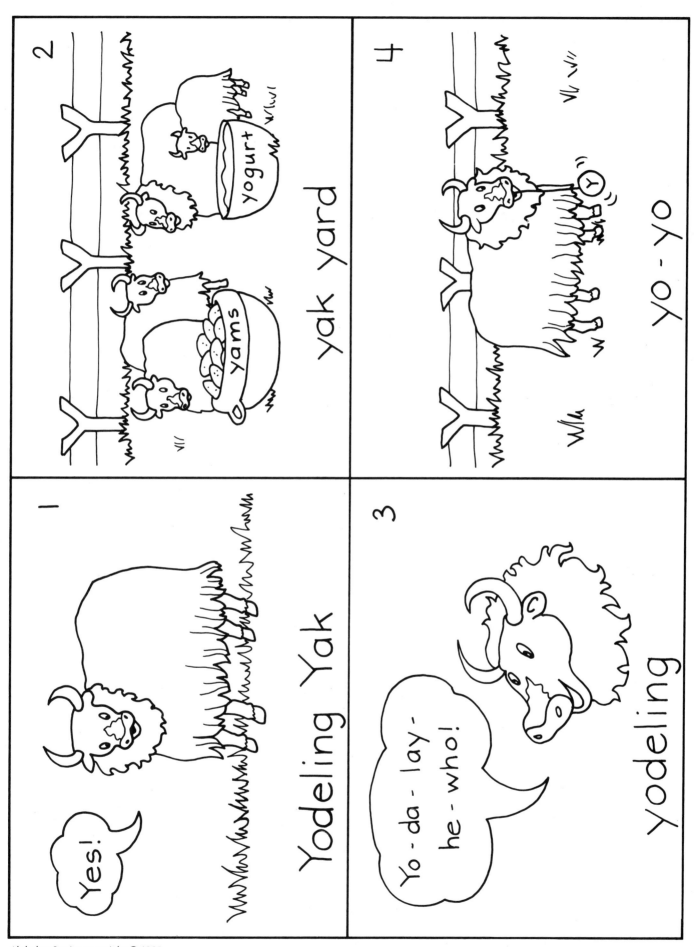

2

Y Y Y

yogurt

yams

yak yard

4

Y Y

Y

yo-yo

1

Yes!

Yodeling Yak

3

Yo - da - lay - he - who!

Yodeling

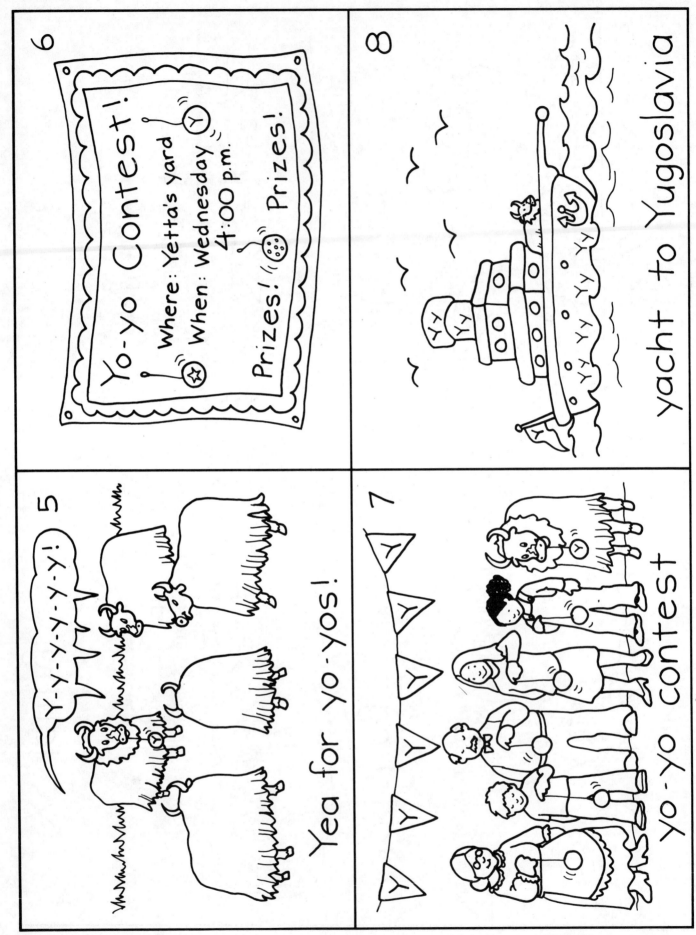

6

Yo-yo Contest!

Where: Yetta's yard
When: Wednesday
4:00 p.m.

Prizes! Prizes!

8

yacht to Yugoslavia

5

Y-Y-Y-Y!

Yea for yo-yos!

7

yo-yo contest

I am Zippy Zebra.

ZIPPY ZEBRA

1. This is the story of Zippy Zebra. She wore a zipper because she loved the sound it made when it went up and down! "ZZZZZ-ZZZZZ-ZZZZZ!"   (*Have the children make the* **Z** *sound with you while pretending to zip.*)

2. Zippy Zebra lived in a zoo. She loved to zip around in her cage at the zoo. Zippy was never still. She was always zooming around!

3. Zeke the zookeeper took care of all the zoo animals. He liked Zippy Zebra the best of all. She was always so happy and zippy. She brightened Zeke's busy days.

4. One day, Zeke had to leave the zoo for an important zoo meeting. He asked Zippy Zebra to take his place as zookeeper and care for the zoo and all the animals while he was away.

5. When Zeke had gone, Zippy zoomed all over the zoo making her zipper go, "ZZZZZ-ZZZZZ-ZZZZZ!" The other animals loved to see Zippy. Zippy began to change a few things about the zoo.

6. She painted special ZIP codes on all the animal cages. Every cage had at least one zero in its ZIP code. Zippy loved the number zero. Can you guess why? The zebra ZIP code was 00000!

7. Zippy planted zinnias around each cage in the zoo. How lovely zinnias are at a zoo! Zippy picked some zinnias and brought them to sick or unhappy animals to cheer them up.

8. Zeke came back to find the zoo changed. He called it a zany zoo. All the animals laughed as Zippy Zebra zipped and zoomed back to her cage: "ZZZZZ-ZZZZZ-ZZZZZ!"

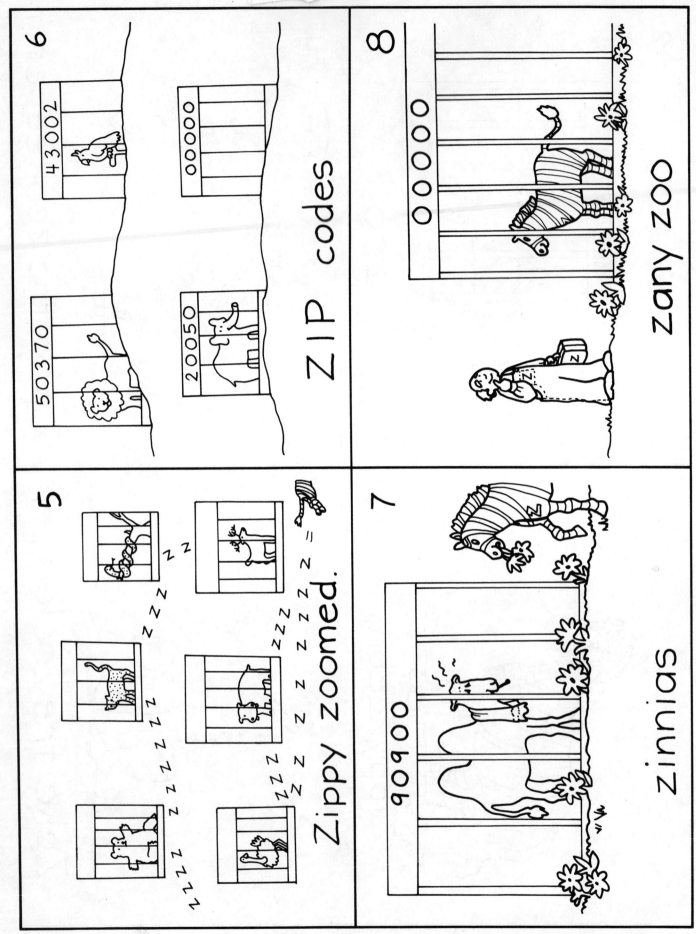

6

43002

50370

20050

00000

ZIP codes

5

Zippy zoomed.

z z z z z z z z z z z z z z z z z z z

8

00000

zany zoo

7

90900

zinnias